Balanced Literacy Instruction: A Teacher's Resource Book

Kathryn H. Au

Jacquelin II. Carroll

Judith A. Scheu

Christopher-Gordon Publishers, Inc.
Norwood, Massachusetts

Credits

Christopher-Gordon Publishers, Inc.
480 Washington Street
Norwood, MA 02062
Tel: 1-800-934-8322

Copyright © 1997 by Christopher-Gordon Publishers, Inc.

10 9 8 7 6 5 4 3 2 1   02 01 00 99 98 97

ISBN: 0-926842-60-9

TABLE OF CONTENTS

challenging or controversial topic, such as phonics, grading, or the instruction of struggling readers. Most chapters also include an article on making connections to the home and community.

The remaining 15 percent of the articles feature the thinking of experts ranging from the Russian psychologist Lev Vygotsky to children's literature expert Violet Harris. We wrote these articles as a way of presenting theories and key concepts in as painless a manner as possible. It is only through theory that the reasons for teaching in one way rather than another become clear. We know, however, that most teachers prefer to start with practice rather than theory, and many may choose to read these "expert" articles last. Many teachers told us that the theory made sense to them only after they had become comfortable with teaching the readers' and writers' workshops. Then the theory became highly valuable, as a way of guiding their instructional decision-making.

Each article, chapter, and section can be read on its own. We designed the book to be used as a resource that teachers might dip into from time to time, reading as much or as little as time and interest permit.

Nevertheless, a few words about the overall structure of our book might be valuable to readers. The book is organized into five sections. The first section, which consists of just one chapter, is an introduction to balanced literacy instruction. It opens with classroom vignettes, followed by an article presenting a curriculum framework for balanced literacy instruction. The rest of the section features the ideas of some of the key figures in the field. Don't be alarmed. This is the only section that consists largely of the "expert" articles mentioned earlier.

The second section focuses on the readers' workshop. This section opens with a chapter showing how the readers' workshop operates in sample classrooms at grades K, 2, and 4. The next chapter explores the structure and organization of the readers' workshop. The last two chapters in this section look at teacher-directed activities and at student-directed activities in the readers' workshop.

The third section addresses the writers' workshop. Like the readers' workshop section, we began this one with an overview, followed by a chapter on structure and organization, followed by chapters on teacher-directed and student-directed activities. We organized the two sections in the same manner in order to show the parallels between the two workshops. In our experience, teachers find it best to begin by implementing just one of the workshops, usually the writers' workshop. Once the first workshop has been implemented, they find it easier to put the second workshop in place, because many of the same principles can be applied.

The fourth section focuses on the all-important topic of assessment and evaluation. Many states, districts, and schools are attempting to promote students' literacy achievement through the implementation of standards, outcomes, or benchmarks. Our treatment of assessment provides practical advice for teachers in these states, districts, and schools. We also discuss student-centered approaches to assessment. This section gives an overview of assessment procedures in sample classrooms, then presents chapters on evaluation in the readers' workshop and the writers' workshop.

The final section is entitled "Keeping It Going" and deals with the process of change. We begin this section with vignettes of teachers engaged in the change process. Then we discuss specific steps that staff developers and groups of teachers might follow to initiate and sustain the process of moving toward balanced literacy instruction. This section might be particularly useful to staff developers, instructional leaders, and others working with the change process. This chapter also provides guidance to teachers who wish to direct their own professional development.

In short, we have tried in this book to bring together the information that we believe teachers need to make balanced literacy instruction a reality in their classrooms. We believe that the systematic application of this knowledge can lead us closer to the goal of helping all students attain the high levels of literacy they deserve and require.

Kathy Au

Jackie Carroll

Judy Scheu

Honolulu, Hawai'i

January, 1997

Chapter 1
PERSPECTIVES

Classroom Vignettes

These vignettes illustrate some of the experiences students are likely to have in classrooms with balanced literacy instruction. The vignettes provide a quick look at the major approaches to be discussed in detail in this book: the process approach to writing and the writers' workshop, and literature-based instruction and the readers' workshop. These vignettes provide a look at balanced instruction from the perspective of the students. The other vignettes in this book approach balanced literacy instruction from the perspective of the teacher.

A Kindergarten Writer Gains Independence

One day in March, Debbie couldn't wait for the writers' workshop to begin, because she had something important to write about. She wrote independently, pronouncing each word and recording letters for the sounds she heard. When she conferred with her teacher, Sally O'Brien, she read the exciting news, pointing to each word:

> I WNT TO SE MY BE nES [I went to see my baby niece]

> AT MY ANTE RNAS HS. [at my Aunty Renee's house.]

After sharing her writing with her teacher, Debbie exclaimed, "Dasherez is her name. I better add that to my story." She returned to her draft and wrote:

> DCRACWZ is r NM. [Dasherez is her name.]

In the days that followed, Debbie added to this draft. When she was finished, Mrs. O'Brien helped her spell the words correctly. Debbie published her story as an illustrated book. She shared her book in the author's chair, and Mrs. O'Brien placed the book in the classroom library so it would be available for the other children to read.

The kindergarten children in this class functioned with remarkable independence during the writers' workshop, because Mrs. O'Brien developed and fostered that independence. For example, she modeled a strategy for sounding out and writing words by leaving spaces in the middle for unknown letters, and she told her students they could do the same in their writing. When Debbie wanted to write *were*, Mrs. O'Brien asked her how she could do that. Debbie wrote the letters *w* and *r*, leaving a space between them. "I'm going to fill it in," she told her teacher. Then she put an e between the other two letters. Mrs. O'Brien showed the class how to use print resources around the room to find the words they needed for their stories. When Debbie needed the word *monster*, Nathan led her to the word charts and began looking through the *m* page with her. Debbie told Nathan, "I can do it myself. I know where to find it."

A Second Grader Makes Reading-Writing Connections

During the writers' workshop, Elaine and Kanani went to an area designated for peer conferences to talk about a piece Elaine had written, a 31/4-page text inspired by the story of Goldilocks and the three bears. Elaine's draft reflected revisions she had made earlier when working on her own. She and Kanani left the area to get a sticker from the table at the front of the room. They returned to the conference table and Elaine wrote the date and their names, then placed the sticker at the bottom of her story as a record of their conference. The children pulled a card from the tub containing guides for conferences and read, "Read story." Elaine began, "Once upon a time...." Soon she stopped and said, "No," crossed out a word and added another. She did this frequently as she continued to read aloud. Kanani played with a sticker but listened attentively. When Elaine occasionally hesitated on a word, he said one aloud that made sense.

Kanani had no questions for Elaine, so they decided their conference was complete. Kanani went to the publishing center and continued working on illustrations for his latest book. Elaine got a copy of *The Three Bears* from the classroom library and took it to her desk. She used it to correct words she had circled in her story, words she thought were spelled incorrectly. She changed *samill* (small) to *wee* and *bag* (big) to *great*.

Elaine said to herself, "Now what I got to do? O.k. I know what to do." She went to the front table and wrote her name in the notebook to show that she was ready for a teacher conference.

During the readers' workshop, Marcus Jamal, Elaine's teacher, had had the students read an assortment of traditional tales. These included stories from the European tradition (such as "Cinderella"), as well as those from Africa (such as *Mufaro's Beautiful Daughters*) and Asia (*Yeh Shen*). After the students had read and enjoyed these stories, Mr. Jamal had them prepare illustrations to add to a story matrix. This activity allowed the students to see similarities and differences among the tales. Mr. Jamal suggested that students might like to try writing their own versions of familiar tales during the writers' workshop. Elaine was one of the students who chose to do so.

A Fourth Grader Responds to Literature

During the readers' workshop, Sol joined a group of five classmates in a circle on the carpet for a literature discussion group. The students were reading *A Taste of Blackberries*, and today it was his turn to lead the discussion. The students began to take turns reading aloud the latest entries written in their literature response logs. Halfway around the circle, Sol stopped the group.

"Do you see what we're doing?" he asked. The others didn't understand what he meant. Sol explained, "We're just reading aloud and we're not talking about anything. Like when Jamie just read, nobody said anything. We're supposed to tell her what we think about what she wrote." Following Sol's suggestion, the students commented on Jamie's written response, saying what they liked about it and whether they had written something similar or different. Gradually, what had begun as a stilted display of reading aloud turned into an animated conversation about the novel.

Sol and the other students in Brenda DeRego's class were given many opportunities to lead their own literature discussion groups. At the beginning of the year, Ms. DeRego taught her students standards for good discussions, so that they learned to value a diversity of ideas and respect each other's opinions. One day, Ms. DeRego spoke with Sol's group about how they could improve their discussions of literature.

"No arguing," Kurt said.

"Yeah, but what if you don't agree with what that person is saying?" Sol wondered.

"If you disagree with someone, how can you say it?" Ms. DeRego asked the group.

"Excuse me, I have another idea," Jamie suggested. Ms. DeRego nodded and emphasized the importance of being able to express a different opinion without hurting someone's feelings. ✳

The Six Aspects of Literacy:
A Curriculum Framework

A balanced approach to literacy instruction calls for a curriculum framework that gives reading and writing equal status. Such a framework recognizes the importance of both the cognitive and affective dimensions of literacy. It acknowledges the meaning-making involved in the full processes of reading and writing, while recognizing the importance of the strategies and skills used by proficient readers and writers.

A curriculum framework with these characteristics is presented in Figure 1.1. This framework can also be called a *whole literacy* curriculum (Au, Scheu, Kawakami, & Herman, 1990). The *whole* part of this label recognizes the importance of students' engagement in the full processes of reading and writing in the authentic contexts for learning provided by the readers' and writers' workshops. The *literacy* part of the label refers to the curriculum's emphasis on reading and writing. Of course, speaking and listening are central to the development of literacy and to activities in the readers' and writers' workshops. Oral language and listening comprehension are fully integrated with reading and writing, since students at all grade levels are expected to share their own ideas and respond to the ideas of others. This approach is consistent with research in emergent literacy, which supports the view that literacy does not wait on oral language development (Teale, 1987).

As shown in Figure 1.1, the overall goal of the curriculum is to promote

Figure 1.1   THE SIX ASPECTS OF LITERACY

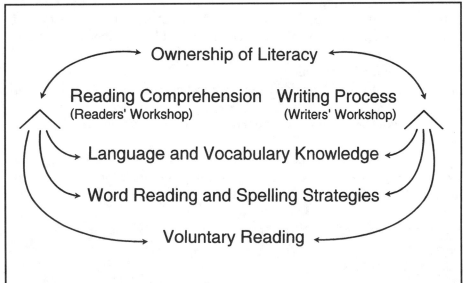

students' ownership of literacy (see Student Ownership, Chapter 5). Ownership involves students' valuing of their own ability to read and write. Students who own literacy are those who choose to use literacy for purposes they have set for themselves, at home as well as at school. For example, students choose to read a book in their spare time or to write a letter to a grandparent. Ownership develops best in classrooms in which students and teachers form a community of learners (Cairney & Langbien, 1989). Students within this community are recognized for their accomplishments as readers and writers and strive to support one another's literacy learning (Blackburn, 1984).

The next two aspects of literacy, reading comprehension and the writing process, are listed below ownership in Figure 1.1. Reading comprehension is at the heart of the readers' workshop, while the writing process serves as the focus for the writers' workshop. The remaining three aspects of literacy—language and vocabulary knowledge, word reading and spelling strategies, and voluntary reading—are all developed within both the readers' and the writers' workshops.

Reading Comprehension

Reading comprehension involves the ability to construct meaning from and to respond to text, using background knowledge as well as printed information. Reading is viewed as the dynamic interaction among the reader, the text, and the situation or social context in which reading takes place (Wixson, Peters, Weber, & Roeber, 1987). In this perspective, a text may have different interpretations, depending on the background knowledge the reader brings to it (Anderson & Pearson, 1984). The social context also influences the process of constructing meaning from text. For example, a reader's interpretation of a novel might differ depending on whether she will be discussing the novel in class or is reading purely for her own enjoyment (Purves, 1985).

Reader response theory (see The Impact of Louise Rosenblatt: Reader Response Theory, Chapter 2) plays an important part in a balanced approach to literacy instruction. According to Rosenblatt (1978), more emphasis needs to be placed on the enjoyment of the reading experience, rather than on reading to gather facts or details from the text. Traditional instruction in reading comprehension was largely based on quizzing students about details in the text. According to Rosenblatt and others, an overemphasis on low-level questions detracts from students' efforts to appreciate the novel or other text as a whole and to draw relationships between the text and their own lives. In keeping with reader response theory, teachers might ask students to discuss their feelings about a text, its possible themes, and connections between the text and their own lives (see Chapter 4).

Writing Process

Writing involves a process of using print (or for younger children, drawing) to construct meaning and communicate a message. Students experience ownership of writing when they write on self-selected topics and come to see themselves as authors. In a balanced literacy curriculum, writing is viewed as a dynamic, nonlinear process. This process includes planning, drafting, revising, editing, and publishing (Graves, 1983; see The Impact of Donald Graves: The Process Approach to Writing, Chapter 6).

Typically, writers go back and forth among these different activities. While drafting, for example, the writer may decide to abandon the piece and begin planning a new one. This thoughtful and deliberate shifting from one activity to another is characteristic of good writers. Good writers pay attention mainly to the overall shape and message of the piece. In contrast, poor writers often become overly concerned with the mechanics of writing, such as spelling and punctuation, rather than with the flow of ideas.

Language and Vocabulary Knowledge

This aspect of literacy concerns students' ability to understand and use appropriate terms and structures in both spoken and printed English. The approach to language development in a balanced literacy curriculum is based on the idea that children learn language by using it for real purposes in social situations (Pinnell & Jaggar, 1991). For example, children can develop oral language through small group, teacher-guided discussions in which they share their responses to an interesting book. Teachers foster children's language development by providing them with many opportunities for authentic communication. Through these opportunities, children gain communicative competence, the ability to use language to express themselves appropriately in a variety of social contexts, and the ability to use language as a tool for learning.

The approach to vocabulary taken in a balanced literacy approach is based on the *knowledge hypothesis* (Mezynski, 1983), the idea that vocabulary represents the knowledge a person has of particular topics, not just dictionary definitions. The meaning of a new word is acquired gradually, through repeated encounters with that word (Nagy, Herman, & Anderson, 1985). Teachers can build students' vocabulary knowledge by heightening their interest in words, by teaching them strategies for inferring word meanings from text, and by encouraging them to do wide independent reading (see Vocabulary Development, Chapter 4).

Word Reading and Spelling Strategies

Many children first learn to deal with print through home experiences with literacy (Taylor, 1983), especially storybook reading. Through storybook reading, children learn concepts about print, for example, that the left page is read before the right and that words run from left to right. Learning concepts about print give children the foundation for developing word reading and spelling strategies.

Students need to have word reading and spelling strategies if they are to read words accurately and quickly. *Fluent readers*, those who experience a smooth and easy flow through the text, integrate knowledge of meaning, structure, and visual cues (Clay, 1993) and decode by analogy (by comparing the unknown word to known words with the same spelling patterns; Cunningham, 1975-1976; see Decoding by Analogy, Chapter 4). Instruction in word reading strategies involves helping students to use the three cue systems mentioned above in a balanced manner. Students must learn to check their guesses about words by using not just one but all three cue systems, and then to correct their guesses. Once students learn to use the three cue systems in a balanced manner, they usually stumble only over multisyllabic words. At this point, they can benefit from learning about base words and affixes, including plural endings, prefixes, and suffixes.

Teachers can help students to develop word reading strategies by teaching them to apply knowledge of the three cue systems when reading (see The Impact of Marie Clay: Cue Systems, Chapter 4). Many students benefit from specific instruction in word reading strategies, including phonics (see Troubleshooting: What About Phonics, Chapter 4). In addition to teaching word reading strategies, teachers can make sure children receive ample opportunity to read and reread favorite books. Through reading and rereading, students learn to apply knowledge of the three cue systems in a fluent, coordinated manner. Writing, especially invented spelling, provides children with an excellent opportunity to learn about sound-symbol relationships (see Troubleshooting: What About Conventional Spelling?, Chapter 8).

Voluntary Reading

In *voluntary reading*, students select the materials they want to read, either for information or for pleasure (Spiegel, 1981). Students read to fulfill their own goals, not just to meet the expectations of the teacher and other adults. Ideally, students choose the times when they will read. Voluntary reading is one way that students demonstrate their ownership of literacy (see Voluntary and Independent Reading, Chapter 5).

Students' voluntary reading is promoted if they become part of a community of readers. In a community of readers, students and teachers give book talks and otherwise share their reading with one another. Students' voluntary reading is supported because they receive recognition and support for their reading and gain ideas about what they would like to read next. Of course, students must also have ready access to books, preferably through an inviting and well stocked classroom library (Morrow & Weinstein, 1986).

Conclusion

In a balanced literacy curriculum, teachers attend to all six aspects of literacy. Two aspects, ownership and voluntary reading, are affective, while the others are cognitive. Two aspects, reading comprehension and the writing process, focus on complex, higher level thinking and meaning making. The final two aspects, language and vocabulary knowledge and word reading and spelling strategies identification, attend to the supporting skills students need to become proficient readers and writers. ✷

References

Anderson, R. C., & Pearson, P. D. (1984). A schema-theoretic view of basic processes in reading comprehension. In P. D. Pearson (Ed.), *Handbook of reading research.* New York, NY: Longman.

Au, K. H., Scheu, J. A., Kawakami, A. J., & Herman, P. A. (1990). Assessment and accountability in a whole literacy curriculum. *The Reading Teacher, 43* (8), 574-578.

Blackburn, E. (1984). Common ground: Developing relationships between reading and writing. *Language Arts, 61,* 367-375.

Cairney, T., & Langbien, S. (1989). Building communities of readers and writers. *The Reading Teacher, 42* (8), 560-567.

Clay, M. M. (1993). *Reading recovery: A guidebook for teachers in training.* Portsmouth, NH: Heinemann.

Cunningham, P. (1975-1976). Investigating a synthesized theory of mediated word recognition. *Reading Research Quarterly, 11,* 127-143.

Graves, D. (1983). *Writing: Teachers and children at work.* Exeter, NH: Heinemann.

Mezynski, K. (1983). Issues concerning the acquisition of knowledge: Effects of vocabulary training on reading comprehension. *Review of Educational Research, 53,* 253-279.

Morrow, L. M., & Weinstein, C. S. (1986). Encouraging voluntary reading: The impact of a literature program on children's use of library centers. *Reading Research Quarterly, 21* (3), 330-346.

Nagy, W. E., Herman, P., & Anderson, R. C. (1985). Learning words from context. *Reading Research Quarterly, 20,* 233-253.

Pinnell, G. S., & Jaggar, A. M. (1991). Oral language: Speaking and listening in the classroom. In J. Flood, J. M. Jensen, D. Lapp, J. R. Squire (Eds.), *Handbook of research on teaching the English language arts* (pp. 691-720). New York, NY: Macmillan.

Purves, A. C. (1985). That sunny dome: Those caves of ice. In C. R. Cooper (Ed.), *Researching response to literature and the teaching of literature: Points of departure* (pp. 54-69). Norwood, NJ: Ablex.

Rosenblatt, L. (1978). *The reader, the text, the poem: The transactional theory of the literary work.* Carbondale: Southern Illinois University Press.

Spiegel, D. L. (1981). *Reading for pleasure: Guidelines.* Newark, DE: International Reading Association.

Taylor, D. (1983). *Family literacy: Young children learning to read and write.*

Portsmouth, NH: Heinemann.

Teale, W. H. (1987). Emergent literacy: Reading and writing development in early childhood. In J. E. Readence & R. S. Baldwin (Eds.), *Research in literacy: Merging perspectives.* Thirty-sixth yearbook of the National Reading Conference (pp. 45-74). Rochester, NY: National Reading Conference.

Wixson, K. K., Peters, C. W., Weber, E. M., & Roeber, E. D. (1987). New directions in statewide reading assessment. *The Reading Teacher, 40* (8), 749-754.

Children's Books Cited

Louie, A. (1982). *Yen-Shen: A Cinderella story from China.* New York, NY: Philomel.

Smith, D. B. (1973). *A taste of blackberries.* New York, NY: HarperCollins

Steptoe, J. (1987) *Mufaro's beautiful daughters.* New York, NY. Lothrop, Lee & Sheperd.

The Impact of Dorothy Strickland:
Balance in Literacy Instruction

Dorothy Strickland (1994; 1994-1995) has worked with many districts, schools, and teachers seeking to make changes in their programs of literacy instruction (Strickland, 1994; 1994-1995). She notes that most teachers are at some point along a continuum of change. They find the process of change challenging, because certain topics in literacy instruction, such as literature-based instruction and phonics, are hotly debated. Many teachers want to come to terms with the issues in order to improve their instruction. Dorothy Strickland advises these teachers to

> ...get in touch with what you believe about teaching and learning. Your belief system provides the foundation for everything you do. Examine it and give it care and nurturing. But always keep the door open for new ideas and insights. (p. 301)

Skills Versus Meaningful Activities

Achieving a balance in literacy instruction sometimes requires that teachers think about both sides of an emotional conflict. An example of such a conflict is that between advocates of skills and advocates of meaningful literacy activities (Strickland, 1994). Advocates of skills believe that phonics, spelling, punctuation, grammar, and other language conventions must be the focus of the literacy curriculum. They argue that these skills must be taught through direct instruction, in a process that involves students in drill and practice. Advocates of meaningful activities think that literacy curriculum should focus on the full processes of reading and writing. They contend that students gain an understanding of these full processes as they engage in meaningful activities such as reading literature and writing about topics of their own choosing.

Teachers striving for a balanced approach recognize the value in both points of view. They realize that many students, particularly those who do not speak standard English as their first language, may benefit from direct instruction in the conventions (Delpit, 1986). However, they also recognize that skill activities in and of themselves are seldom instrinsically motivating to students. To help students see the purposes of skills, teachers have skill instruction grow out of meaningful literacy activities. For example, a phonics lesson on the sound of *w* can follow the reading of *Whistle for Willie* (Keats, 1964). Similarly, a lesson on beginning sentences with capital letters can occur when students are ready to edit the drafts of the stories they have written. Strickland (1994-95) advises:

> *Don't waste time debating whether or not to teach phonics, spelling, grammar, and other "skills" of literacy.* Obviously, young children cannot read or write without encountering the use of phonics, gram-

mar, spelling, and other conventions of written language. Do spend time discussing how to teach them in a way that contributes to the learners' self-improvement. Keep in mind that these conventions and enablers to reading and writing are not reading and writing nor are they precursors to involvement in reading and writing as meaningful acts. (p. 299; italics in original)

Strickland asks educators to rethink the whole issue of ability grouping. In her opinion, the disadvantages of fixed ability groups far outnumber the advantages. Ability grouping lowers the self-esteem of struggling readers and results in these students receiving far less instruction than they need. In contrast to fixed ability groups, flexible skills groups (see Troubleshooting: What About Phonics?, Chapter 4) give teachers the opportunity to provide intensive skill instruction to those who need it, without creating a permanent "low group" in the classroom.

In balanced literacy instruction, students are given the chance to learn through both direct and indirect instruction. Direct instruction occurs in mini-lessons during the Readers' and Writers' Workshops (see Mini-lessons, Chapters 4 and 8). Indirect instruction and opportunities for discovery occur as students are involved in the full processes of reading and writing, and teachers respond to "teachable moments" in small group and individual instruction. With both direct and indirect instruction, Strickland points out, it is important to recognize the difference between what teachers teach and what students learn.

The Curriculum Versus Students' Needs

Strickland (1994-95) considers the tension between the set curriculum versus students' needs and interests. Teachers may be directed to follow a curriculum from the district, school, or basal reading program. Yet the curriculum may not match teachers' knowledge of their students and what it makes sense to teach at a given moment. Strickland advises teachers to refer to curriculum guides to understand the expectations at their grade level, but not to feel obligated to teach the skills in the exact order in which they appear in the guides. In balanced literacy instruction, skills are developed in an ongoing way. As Strickland points out, it is not a matter of checking off a skill such as "sequence of events" and moving on to the next skill. A skill such as identifying the sequence of events may be taught, applied, and reviewed on a number of occasions, with increasingly complex texts.

Structures for Literacy Instruction

Strickland makes the following suggestions to teachers engaged in changing the way they teach literacy. First, she suggests, teachers should work together to establish structures for planning and organizing instruction. Skillful teachers, Strickland writes, establish predictable schedules and

The Impact of Lev Vygotsky: Social Constructivism

A logical starting point for a discussion of literacy instruction is the question of how people learn to read and write, or of how people learn, in general. *Constructivism* and *social constructivism* are philosophical views that challenge traditional views about learning. The thinking of the Russian psychologist Lev Vygotsky (1896-1934) has contributed greatly to the development of constructivist views within the field of literacy instruction.

The traditional view is that the learner is a passive recipient of knowledge. In this view, the learner may be compared to a blank tablet, and the teacher's job may be compared to filling the tablet with writing. The constructivist view is quite different. According to this view, learners actively construct or create their own understandings. Students do not learn simply because teachers tell them something (for example, that plants need light to grow). They learn when they have the opportunity to engage with the new ideas and make them their own (for example, by seeing for themselves what happens when plants are kept in the closet).

As its name suggests, social constructivism differs from "just plain" constructivism in emphasizing the social world surrounding the learner. Earlier forms of constructivism (for example, as seen in the work of the famous developmental psychologist Jean Piaget) tended to see learning mainly as a matter of changes that took place within the learner. In social constructivism, learning is not seen only in terms of the individual. Rather, learning is seen in terms of the interactions of the individual with other people.

Importance of the Social World

Vygotsky's work has done much to bring the social aspect of social constructivism to the attention of educators. One of the major themes in Vygotsky's work is the idea that complex types of human activity, such as language and literacy, begin in the social world (Wertsch, 1990). Vygotsky argues that the individual's first attempts at complex types of activity, such as speech, are carried out with social support from other people. When a baby babbles, "Wah-wah," her mother may help by saying, "Water, do you want water?" Over time, the child takes over more and more responsibility for speaking, until he can speak independently. As the child does more, the adult can do less. There is a gradual release of responsibility from the adult to the child.

In the same way, literacy begins as a social activity between the child and adult. For example, a child may be able to write at first only when an adult helps him put his ideas into words and write the words down on paper. Gradually, as the child learns the strategies and skills of planning and drafting his writing independently, less and less adult help is required.

In Vygotsky's view, the key to learning does not lie in the child's innate ability (Moll, 1990). Rather, the key to learning is the social support the child receives from adults or peers. Differences in literacy achievement are not simply the result of some children having more ability than others. Children's success or failure in learning to read and write, Vygotsky's thinking suggests, can best be understood by examining the social world in which their learning is taking place. Differences in achievement have probably come about because of differences in the literacy instruction and experiences students have received.

Zone of Proximal Development

In Vygotsky's thinking about how people learn, *the zone of proximal development* is a central concept. Vygotsky states that the zone represents the "difference between the child's actual level of development and the level of performance that he achieves in collaboration with the adult" (Vygotsky, 1987, p. 209). The zone is the region of sensitivity to instruction.

The learning the child is doing, or the new level of performance the child is attempting, must be in the zone of proximal development. Below the zone, the child will not learn anything new, because the level of performance is too easy. For example, a kindergarten child who can read simple, predictable books probably will not benefit from prolonged instruction in reading similar books. Beyond the zone, the child will not benefit either, because the level of performance demanded is too difficult. For example, the same kindergarten child probably will not benefit from instruction in reading a chapter book with few pictures, because these books are far too difficult.

To help the child learn, the teacher or peer must engage him in a performance of just the right degree of difficulty. In this case, the teacher may make the decision to work with the child on picture books that do not have such predictable text. This decision takes the child to a higher level of performance. However, the child can be successful at this level, with the teacher's assistance.

In Vygotsky's view, if children are to learn, they must have the opportunity to try out the new level of performance with the assistance of someone who knows more than they do. This "more knowledgeable other" may be an adult, or it may be a capable peer. The teacher or peer must provide just the right amount of help. More help is needed at first, and less help is needed later, when the child has become more proficient. When the amount of help changes in this way, to match the needs of the learner, the process is called *scaffolding*. Scaffolding is a temporary kind of help, to be removed when the learner no longer needs it.

Full Processes

Vygotsky's approach to learning is a holistic one. He believed that complex forms of thinking, such as reading and writing, needed to be viewed in a holistic manner, in terms of the full processes involved. Reading and writing and complex forms of thinking involve much more than the accumulation of many simple skills. The skills have to be used in their proper time and place, as part of a complicated process. It is this whole complicated process that children must learn. This view implies that students will learn literacy best by engaging in authentic literacy activities, not isolated skill activities (Moll, 1990). Literacy learning activities should involve the full processes of reading and writing, and skills can be taught as part of students' involvement in these full processes.

The terms *sociocultural* or *sociohistorical* are sometimes used to describe Vygotsky's view, because he believed that culture and history both play a role in learning. When we look at children's literacy learning, Vygotsky's thinking suggests, we have to consider the broader cultural and historical context surrounding their learning. For example, children from some cultural groups grow up speaking standard English at home. Children from other cultural groups grow up speaking Spanish or a nonmainstream variety of English, such as Black English. These cultural groups have unique histories within the United States. Vygotsky's ideas suggest that educators must take a broad view of the factors influencing learning.

Research conducted from a social constructivist perspective highlights the fact that schools present children who speak different languages or come from different cultural backgrounds with different opportunities for learning. In general, schools are more successful with mainstream students who speak standard English as a first language than with other students. Vygotsky's thinking implies that teachers should be aware of the cultural and historical factors that affect students' opportunity to learn, and of ways to adjust the classroom environment and systems of instruction to enable students to be successful in learning to read and write.

In Vygotsky's view, language and literacy are not fixed entities. Instead, Vygotsky saw language and literacy as human inventions. These inventions developed over time to help people coordinate their interactions with the physical world and with each other (Cole, 1990). Language and literacy, like other human inventions, change to meet different purposes at different times. For example, over the past decade people have invented and brought into common English usage terms for the computer's many parts and accessories. In connection with the computer, people have begun to develop new forms of literacy, such as writing messages for electronic mail.

In short, the social constructivist perspective and the work of Vygotsky present literacy educators with many new ideas. Perhaps most importantly, this perspective suggests that children of all linguistic and cultural backgrounds can achieve high levels of literacy, if educators understand how to adjust the learning environment to support their learning. ✳

References

Code, M. (1990). Cognitive development and schooling: The evidence from cross-cultural research. In L. C. Moll (Ed.), *Vygotsky and education: Instructional implications and applications of sociohistorical psychology* (pp. 89-110). Cambridge, MA: Cambridge University Press.

Moll, L. C. (1990). Introduction. In L. C. Moll (Ed.), *Vygotsky and education: Instructional implications and applications of sociohistorical psychology* (pp. 1-27). Cambridge, MA: Cambridge University Press.

Vygotsky, L. S. (1978). *Mind in society.* Cambridge, MA: Harvard University Press.

Wertsch, J. V. (1990). The voice of rationality in a sociocultural approach to mind. In L. C. Moll (Ed.), *Vygotsky and education: Instructional implications and applications of sociohistorical psychology* (pp. 111-126). Cambridge, MA: Cambridge University Press.

Chapter 2

OVERVIEW OF THE READERS' WORKSHOP

Reader's Workshop in
Mrs. Sally O'Brien's Kindergarten Class

Mrs. Sally O'Brien's kindergarten class is learning about farms and farm animals. The topic gives the teacher and students a focus for reading, sharing their ideas, follow-up assignments, activities, and projects. Earlier this week the class visited a farm where the students saw chickens laying eggs. Currently the class has a project hatching chicken eggs in an incubator.

With the class sitting together on the carpet, Mrs. O'Brien begins the reading instruction by writing a message on the whiteboard.

Good morning boys and girls,
The chicks have started to hatch! Two eggs have
little cracks. Soon we will see the baby chicks.

As the children observe her writing, they spontaneously try to read along. Then Mrs. O'Brien and the students read the message together. They discuss the news and share the excitement. Leanne exclaims, "I hear a little peep." The children help Mrs. O'Brien add that sentence to the message by listening for the sounds in the words and suggesting letters for the sounds. The children can supply most of the consonants and a few of the vowels. Brian notices the word "little" is already in the message and Mrs. O'Brien praises him for "having good eyes."

She then focuses their attention on the whole message and asks the

again. The group discusses the picture, pointing out some of the details and then makes predictions about what might go in the soup. Mrs. O'Brien begins reading, pointing to each word as she reads. The students recognize the pattern and read along. For their follow-up assignment the students will draw and label some things they saw growing on the farm that could be used to make soup.

The classroom activities support study of the farm and provide other literacy opportunities. The library center has lots of trade books and a special collection of books about farm animals and life on a farm. There are stories published by students and books the class published together. The block area has toy farm animals for use with block construction. There is a box with construction paper and markers for the students to make labels and signs. The housekeeping area has been converted into a roadside restaurant featuring home-cooked meals with fresh produce from the farm. There are menus to read and paper and pencils to write orders. The listening post has a tape of *The Duck Who Loved Puddles* (1986) and copies of the books by Michael J. Pellowski so students can follow along as they listen to the story.

Before the end of readers' workshop, Mrs. O'Brien tells the class she will read aloud Margot Zemach's *The Little Red Hen* (1983). This is a different version of the story than she chooses for small group instruction. After reading the story Mrs. O'Brien allows time for the students to talk about story ideas and events and to ask and respond to questions. ❋

Children's Books Cited

Cowley, J. (1990). *Farm concert*. Bothell, WA: The Wright Group.

Cowley, J. (1986). *Yuk soup*. Illustrated by R. McRae. Bothel, WA: The Wright Group.

Galdone, P. (1973). *Little red hen*. Jefferson City, MO: Scholastic.

Hodder, W. III. (1988). *Five little chickens*. Cleveland, OH: Modern Curriculum Press.

Pellowski, M. J. (1986). *The duck who loved puddles*. Illustrated by D. Paterson. Mahwah, NJ: Troll Associates.

Zemach, M. (1983). *The little red hen*. East Rutherford, NJ: Farrar, Straus.

Readers' Workshop in
Mr. Marcus Jamal's Second-Grade Class

Mr. Marcus Jamal's second-grade class is learning about friendship. This theme gives the teacher and students a focus for reading, writing, and discussing their ideas during readers' workshop. Mr. Jamal begins the workshop today with OTTER (Our Time to Enjoy Reading). The children and Mr. Jamal independently read from books they have selected until the timer sounds after 20 minutes. Then, for about 10 minutes, they talk about their books. Today Mr. Jamal asks, "Who was reading a book in which friendships are important? Will you tell us a little about those friendships?"

After several children have shared, Mr. Jamal spends about 5 minutes conducting a mini-lesson on a procedure he wants the class to learn—how to discuss a story in a small group independently of the teacher. He wants them to practice sharing their ideas with their peers and begin to develop independence in story discussions. He explains how one person brings up a topic (what she thinks about a character's actions, or how a certain part confused her) and other people listen and respond to it for a while before someone else brings up another topic. Students will practice this procedure later in the day.

The class has four reading groups, formed on the basis of both interest and reading ability. Each group meets daily with Mr. Jamal for about 20 minutes. Two groups are reading *Katy No-Pocket* by Emmy Payne (1944), but each group meets separately for discussion to keep the groups small. When one of these groups meets with Mr. Jamal he begins by having the students share their current response journal entries and inviting comments from the group. As they read and discuss the next section of the book together, he uses the ETR approach (see Experience-Text-Relationship Lessons, Chapter 4) to help students relate their prior knowledge and experiences to new text ideas.

Mr. Jamal asks the group to share any new or interesting vocabulary they have noted in their response journals as they read. One child has written the phrase *squatting-down*. The group discusses the meaning, using information from the context, including picture cues, as well as visual and structural cues. Mr. Jamal uses this opportunity to talk about root words and endings, helping the group find other words with endings (*crying, cried, rising, squatted, sensible, kindly*) and figure out their roots.

Mr. Jamal determined that students in the other group reading *Katy No-Pocket* could benefit from more guidance with their written response. Their responses are written on an open-ended response sheet that he designed (see Figure 2.2).

Another group is reading *Frog and Toad Together* by Arnold Lobel (1971). They are sitting together to reread a section they read and discussed

Readers' Workshop in
Ms. Brenda DeRego's Fourth-Grade Class

Ms. Brenda DeRego, a fourth-grade teacher, began the school year by asking her students to think and write about their previous accomplishments in reading and set goals for themselves for the first quarter. After discussion, the students decided to add work samples to their portfolios at least once a month, and to look over their goals and review their progress monthly.

For the first 20 minutes of class after morning business, students read independently a book of their choice and record it in their reading logs (see Voluntary and Independent Reading, Chapter 5). Ms. DeRego reads along with her students. Available are text sets and author sets that have been gathered by classroom librarians. This quarter they include text sets on family relationships (the theme related to their literature study groups) and author sets by Katherine Paterson and Patricia MacLachlan (authors they are reading in literature discussion groups).

On Mondays, Ms. DeRego collects the reading logs, which include students' comments and a parent's signature. Once a month, Ms. DeRego asks the students to complete a book project. Some students create book jackets, some do dioramas, some make mobiles or posters, and others dress as a character and give a presentation to the class.

Ms. DeRego often uses literature she has been reading aloud as a model in her mini-lessons. Today she spends about 20 minutes reading from *The Star Fisher* by Lawrence Yep (1991) and discussing how readers develop a sense of theme through character actions and thoughts. She has chosen this topic because the literature study groups have finished or are nearly finished with their novels and she wants to give them ways to explore themes.

There are four literature study groups reading one of two books on family relationships: *The Great Gilly Hopkins* by Katherine Paterson (1978) or *Journey* by Patricia MacLachlan (1991). Students chose the book they wanted to read after hearing Ms. DeRego's book talks and looking through the books themselves.

The groups meet every two to three days for discussion. On other days, they read and write in their response journals (see Figure 2.3). The groups decide how much they will read before their next meeting together. The groups meet at the same time, with a student serving as facilitator in each group. Earlier in the school year more of the discussions were teacher led. Now Ms. DeRego finds she can move from group to group, listening, making notes, asking questions, and contributing her own ideas to the discussion.

One of the groups reading *Journey* is discussing a *think question* (a question not directly answered in the text, requiring students to engage in reasoning and interpretation) posed by one of the students: Why was it important for Journey to have a sister like Cat? They will also share personal connections they made to the story, vocabulary words, and sparkling jewels (see Vocabulary Development, Chapter 4) from their response journals.

Ms. DeRego is meeting with one of the groups that has finished *The Great Gilly Hopkins*. She is using ETR (see Experience-Text-Relationship Lessons, Chapter 4) to have students discuss their feelings about the book's ending, their ideas about the author's message, and their personal evaluations of the book.

After this 40-minute period for literature discussion groups, Ms. DeRego reserves another 10 minutes for pulling things together. Sometimes she asks the students to evaluate how well they have been working individually and in groups. She reminds them to think about their goals and the progress they are making. They write first and then share their evaluations. She uses this time to help them identify and solve problems related to working in groups.

At other times the class talks about the relationships between the books they are reading in literature groups and others related to the theme they are exploring. Students have a chance to compare and contrast characters and themes from different books. Often, as a result of these discussions, students decide to read a book someone else has been reading. ✳

Figure 2.3   FOURTH-GRADE STUDENT'S RESPONSE TO LITERATURE

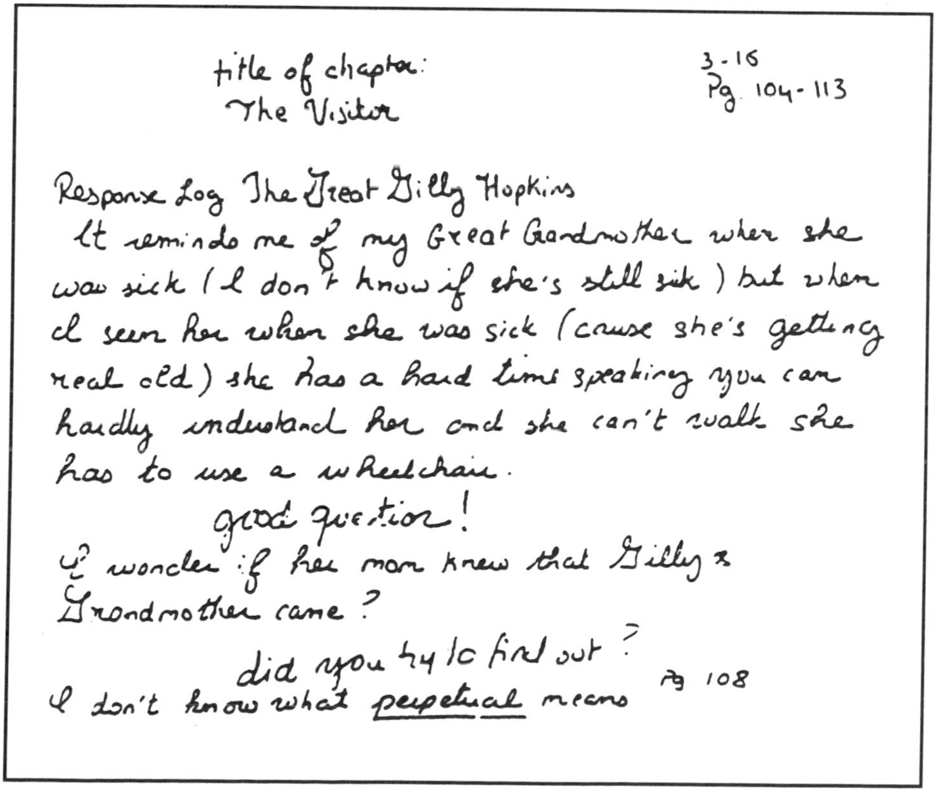

title of chapter:
The Visitor

3-15
Pg. 104-113

Response Log The Great Gilly Hopkins
It reminds me of my Great Grandmother when she was sick (I don't know if she's still sik) but when I seen her when she was sick (cause she's getting real old) she has a hard time speaking you can hardly understand her and she can't walk she has to use a wheelchair.
        good question!
I wonder if her mom knew that Gilly & Grandmother came?
            did you try to find out?   Pg 108
I don't know what perpetual means

Procedure

Principles such as those cited by Hansen call for a classroom that is organized to promote active participation, independence, and interdependence on the part of students (see classroom descriptions in Chapter 2 for more specifics). How teachers set up their classrooms communicates these underlying principles to students. As much as possible, planning should be done jointly by the students and the teacher. Students are often a good source of information about routines that make it easier for the class to operate smoothly.

A well-stocked classroom library is the cornerstone of the readers' workshop, since selecting and reading books will occupy much of students' time. For younger students, books will be more accessible when arranged on shelves with the book covers facing out. Kindergarten teacher Mrs. O'Brien grouped some titles by her favorite authors (Cynthia Rylant, Aliki, and Byrd Baylor) and some by subjects she liked (ocean animals, faraway places, special people), which she placed in labeled bins on tables nearby students' desks. Later, she asked the students to choose their favorite authors and special subjects, and to help her restock and relabel the bins.

For older students, fiction and nonfiction can be grouped separately, alphabetized with spines out. Ms. DeRego's fourth graders made large bookmarks with their names on them that they used to mark the place on the shelf for the book they borrowed. Titles could be reshelved easily when students were finished with their books. Like the younger students, these students still enjoyed making special book displays to feature favorite authors and subjects.

Book titles should be rotated regularly. Some teachers borrow from school or community libraries or exchange with other classrooms. Student-authored books can be shelved with the regular collection or kept in a special display area within the library. Other reading material such as newspapers, magazines, and reference books make up part of the collection. Parents may be willing to donate books and magazines their child no longer needs at home. Teachers can create a comfortable place for students to browse, read on their own, or pair up to enjoy books together by adding a carpet and some large cushions to the library area.

A system for borrowing books to take home should be set up so that students can manage it, perhaps by posting a sign-out sheet and assigning one or two classroom librarians on a rotating basis to check in books on due days. Some teachers of younger children ask them to bring back their books each day, even though the same book can be checked out again for that night. Teachers of older children may require students to bring back books once a week, allowing them to borrow the same book for a second week if they want to renew it.

A large area where the entire class can gather for discussions and sharing, as well as several areas for small groups to meet, is important for creating a supportive community atmosphere. The whole class can meet at an open area, either sitting on the floor or pulling their chairs together in a circle. One teacher arranged students' desks in a squared-off C shape, using the open area in the middle for mini-lessons and having students sit around the perimeter for sharing. Small groups can meet at desks clustered together or at work tables stationed at the back and sides of the room.

Charts, bulletin boards, and displays can contribute greatly to the smooth running of the readers' workshop. For example, Ms. DeRego began a chart during a mini-lesson on how to figure out unknown words, brainstorming with students to produce a list of strategies. The chart was posted for reference and the teacher and other students encouraged anyone who was stuck in their reading to refer to the chart for help. Ms. DeRego used other charts to list possible discussion questions and different types of responses to literature students might want to try.

Bulletin boards can be used to remind students of the daily schedule of activities for readers' workshop, using pictures and simple labels for younger students. Displays might give information about the Author of the Week, including a special collection of the author's books. This could be a student author or a commercially published author. Students should have many opportunities to design displays and bulletin boards to share information of importance to them in their learning. They may want to create displays for their favorite books or authors, set up a book swap table, or post book recommendations for their classmates.

Teachers can use mini-lessons to explain the classroom set-up to students and to help them operate within this environment. Students learn their responsibilities for using their time productively, making good choices, and interacting with their teacher and classmates in ways that support their learning and the classroom community. Teachers monitor the operation of the classroom and look for ways to refine any parts that are not running smoothly. They discuss possible changes with students and ask for students' ideas about how to make the classroom function better. Students and teachers working together can create an environment that fosters learning. Figure 3.1 gives a sample layout that teachers may find useful when considering how to set up their classrooms. ❄

Reference

Hansen, J. (1987). *When writers read.* Portsmouth, NH: Heinemann.

Figure 3.2

READERS' AND WRITERS' WORKSHOP
SCHEDULE—SECOND GRADE

Figure 3.3

READERS' AND WRITERS' WORKSHOP
SCHEDULE—SIXTH GRADE

Readers' Workshop

Writers' Workshop

8:30 Silent or partner reading

8:50 Book sharing (whole class)

9:00 Mini-lesson—Plurals with -es & -ies

9:10 Teacher meets with:

    Henry and Mudge—Mon. & Thurs.

    Arthur's April Fool—Mon. & Thurs.

    Freckle Juice—Tues. & Fri.

    Best Friends—Tues. & Fri.

    Flexible skills groups—Wed.

10:00 Recess

When your group isn't meeting:

• write in your response journals

• keep reading

• work on your book project

• choose something else related to reading

10:30 Read aloud—*Runaway Ralph*

10:50 Mini-lesson—Noticing details

11:00 Independent writing

    Conferences (teacher and peer)

11:30 Sharing

Sign up if you:

• need a conference

• need editing help

• are ready to share (Author's Chair)

Readers' Workshop

Period 3 10:15 a.m.—11:00 a.m.

Mon.—Wed.

Silent reading and response journals—30 min.

Class sharing, book talks—15 min.

Tues.—Thurs.

Mini-lesson & read aloud—15 min.

Literature discussion groups—30 min.

Fri.

Choice time—30 min.

Class sharing, weekly reflection—15 min.

Writers' Workshop

Period 4 11:05 a.m.—11:50 a.m.

Mon.—Wed.

Mini-lesson—10 min.

Writing and conferring—35 min.

Tues.—Thurs.

Writing and conferring—35 min.

Sharing—10 min.

Fri.

Writing and conferring—30 min.

Class sharing, weekly reflection—15 min.

Grouping

Students routinely have been grouped for reading instruction on the basis of reading ability as measured by standardized test scores, informal reading measures, or their previous year's reading group placement. In readers' workshop classrooms, however, students are grouped for reading instruction according to both needs and interests. *Heterogeneous groups* accommodate students who, regardless of reading level, are excited about reading a story or novel with their friends or are eager to do research with a group by reading about some aspect of the topic and sharing their findings. *Homogeneous* groups are useful for instructing students with similar skill needs. Group membership changes with changing interests and needs.

Background

The composition of reading groups and the effects on readers have been studied extensively by researchers (e.g., Allington & Walmsley, 1995; Gamoran, 1992; Slavin, 1989). Within-class ability grouping in one or two subjects, when students were grouped heterogeneously at other times, were found beneficial in some studies. When students were grouped by ability consistently, however, low groups fell further behind each year. Researchers concluded that instructional differences played a part. Students in high groups received fast-paced, challenging instruction. They focused more on silent reading, comprehension, and high-level thinking skills. Those in low groups got slower-paced, less challenging instruction consisting of more skill sheets, practice drills, and low-level discussion questions.

Mason and Au (1990) recommend alternatives to the sole use of ability groups. They suggest:

- balancing the use of heterogeneous and homogeneous groups,

- using cooperative learning groups,

- working to improve the status of students in low groups, and

- evaluating students on multiple dimensions—for example, special reading talents such as a flair for noticing and using new and interesting vocabulary.

Procedure

Teachers begin the school year by finding out about their students' reading interests, habits, and attitudes. This may take the form of interviews, surveys, observations as students read and talk about books, and/or observations as teachers read aloud to their students. From this information, some teachers select one book the whole class will read and discuss together.

Either following this experience or instead of it, teachers may select three or four books for literature study around a theme of interest to the students and relevance to the curriculum. Later, students may suggest books they want to read together.

Teachers have found that groups of no more than eight allow each student ample opportunity to be heard. Teachers who are more comfortable having fewer stories to keep track of at any one time may have more than one group read the same book. Literature discussion groups are still kept small (about six to eight students per group), so that there may be two or more small groups discussing the same book.

Book talks are used to introduce the selections, which are left out a few days for students to browse through and consider. Teachers will want to talk about how challenging each book may be to read. For example, a book with a great deal of specialized vocabulary may be more difficult for students with no background in the area and easier for students with relevant background. Some children are more comfortable with books that have larger type, more illustrations, shorter sentences, fewer words on a page, or shorter chapters. The teacher can alert students to these features in the books students will choose from.

After students have had time to consider the possibilities, they make first and second choices (see Figure 3.4 for a sample form). The teacher then assigns a book after weighing their preferences, reading level, background knowledge, and level of difficulty of the book. Teachers also consider the strong motivation students have for reading a more challenging book that is of personal interest to them. Even after students have begun their books, the teacher gives them a few days to change their selections if the text proves too difficult or not of interest. When the students finish their books, they can evaluate how well they handled the reading. This information is helpful to the teacher as well as the student when choosing books in the future. Over time, students may be able to choose their own books with little or no assistance from the teacher (see Figure 3.5).

Along with heterogeneous grouping, teachers use homogeneous groups to address specific areas of need. For example, after observing several students struggle repeatedly with unknown words, Mr. Jamal decided to have these students meet with him for a few sessions to explore strategies for figuring out unknown words. This flexible skills group was not a permanent "remedial" group, and the students in it also were members of heterogeneous literature discussion groups. New flexible skills groups can be formed and dissolved as needs arise and are met.

Students just beginning to read usually are placed in homogeneous groups in order to help them interact with text that is challenging but not frustrating. Keeping in mind alternatives for grouping, these students should be placed in different groups for other small group work. For example, students in Mrs. O'Brien's kindergarten class work in heterogeneous small groups on book projects based on favorite stories that have been read aloud.

Following Mason and Au's suggestions, teachers will want to work to improve the status of children perceived as less successful readers and capitalize on their strengths. For example, during class discussions Mr. Jamal calls on struggling readers as often as he does strong readers. He knows that students called on by teachers are perceived as smarter and more knowledgeable by their peers. Since he generally asks open-ended questions, low-achieving readers have equal opportunities to share their insights and contribute thoughtful responses to discussions.

Figure 3.4   SAMPLE FORM FOR STUDENT BOOK SELECTION

Name _____ Date_____

What book would you like to read?

    Best Friends

    Henry and Mudge

    Freckle Juice

    Arthur's April Fool

Write your 1st and 2nd choices.

1st _____

2nd _____

Figure 3.5   TEACHER'S NOTE TO STUDENTS FOR SUGGESTING BOOKS

Dear 6th Graders,

Since our theme is survival, be on the lookout for good novels for our literature discussion groups that will start next week. Someone suggested *Homecoming* by Cynthia Voigt, and there's a group that wants to talk about Gary Paulsen's *Dogsong*. Be ready with ideas when we meet Friday morning.

           Mrs. Okamoto

In addition, Mr. Jamal notes and praises other strengths these students have. One of his students consistently notices when special vocabulary words in their book have been used in other stories the class has heard or read. Another student knows a lot about taking care of pets and applies his knowledge to a discussion of Arthur's *Pet Business* (Brown, 1990). Teachers who work to balance students' instructional needs with their needs for social acceptance and status find that students become more willing collaborators in their own learning. ❋

References

Allington, R. L., & Walmsley, S. A. (Eds.). (1995). *No quick fix: Rethinking literacy programs in America's elementary schools.* Newark, DE: International Reading Association.

Gamoran, A. (1992). Is ability grouping equitable? *Educational Leadership, 50* (2), 11-17.

Mason, J. M., & Au, K. H. (1990). *Reading instruction for today.* New York, NY: HarperCollins.

Slavin, R. E. (1989, September). Synthesis of research on grouping in elementary and secondary schools. *Educational Leadership*, 67-77.

Children's Books Cited

Brown, M. (1990). *Arthur's pet business.* New York, NY: Little Brown.

Selecting Literature

Literature, according to children's literature professor Rebecca Lukens, may be defined as "the body of writing that exists because of inherent imaginative and artistic qualities" (1990, p. 3). We read literature basically for pleasure, she asserts, echoing Louise Rosenblatt's belief that children should read primarily for the aesthetic experience. Selecting good literature—books that contain imaginative and artistic qualities—and promoting children's enjoyment of good literature are at the heart of a strong readers' workshop.

Background

What constitutes good literature, literature that is important and worthy of children's time and attention? Much discussion on this issue has involved attempts to define a literary *canon*: an authoritative list of works to be read by all students. In his research, Alan Purves (1993) explores a canon's underlying purposes: to communicate cultural values and promote cultural identity. Of course, there are many canons, based on beliefs as diverse as the groups that devise them. As values change, canons are modified. The "classics" of the 1950s were largely from the Western European tradition; in the 1990s, we recognize a far greater ethnic diversity and the influence of that diversity on American culture. Native American, African American, Hispanic, and Asian authors and books are now represented in multicultural canons. Yet there is still little consensus as to what belongs in any canon.

Purves suggests that literature in the curriculum goes beyond the literary canon. In order to select literature "with a full respect for the diverse groups that comprise our society" (p. 105), he proposes teachers choose a broad variety of texts, sometimes grouped by cultures, but other times grouped in other ways. For example, to help students understand cultures other than their own, teachers might select a group of books about a specific culture. To help students understand that certain values are universal, teachers might choose a group of books that show the importance of families and friendships in several cultures. In all cases, books should be linked to information about the authors themselves—including the cultures in which they live and work—to enrich the literary experience.

Procedure

Teachers looking for a wide variety of texts will have no shortage from which to choose. The number of titles currently available may make the task seem daunting at first; a working knowledge of children's literature takes time to build. Browsing in the school library, community library, bookstores, and other teachers' classrooms is a good way to start. Libraries and publishers make available helpful book lists. For example, there are lists of

The Impact of Violet Harris:
Multicultural Children's Literature

While teachers continue to share old favorites such as *Charlotte's Web* (White, 1952) during the readers' workshop, they are also finding new favorites such as *Grandfather's Journey* (Say, 1993) in the growing body of multicultural literature. Noting that the term *multicultural literature* appears more and more frequently in discussions of children's literature, Violet Harris (1992a) offers the following definition:

> Multicultural literature refers to literature that focuses on people of color—African, Asian, Hispanic, and Native American; religious minorities, such as the Amish or Jewish; regional cultures, for example, Appalachian and Cajun; the disabled; and the aged. To some extent, the term encompasses literature that presents women and girls in a multitude of roles that are not gender stereotyped. The element common to each group member is its marginal status and its lack of full participation in "mainstream" institutions. (p. 171)

Harris, who conducts research on African American children's literature (1992b), argues for the place of literature focusing on African, Asian, Hispanic, and Native Americans. In the past, works featuring these groups did not find their way into the curriculum. Harris points out that the exclusion of these works prevents students from gaining a broader perspective, because race and ethnicity can serve as lenses through which experiences and history receive different interpretations.

Culturally Conscious Literature

Sims (1982) developed the term *culturally conscious literature* to refer to works that depict the culture of a particular group from the perspective of an insider. Through the author's portrayal of language, traditions, settings, and physical appearances, the reader understands that the characters are African, Asian, Hispanic, or Native American. The author presents the culture in a sensitive and authentic manner, showing the characters as complex individuals rather than as stereotypes. For example, in the Newbery Award winner *Roll of Thunder, Hear My Cry*, Mildred Taylor (1976) tells the story of the Logans, an African American family living in the south in the 1930s. Taylor presents Cassie and her siblings as distinct personalities, growing up in a family with strong principles.

Taylor composes realistic works that include acts of violence against African Americans. Harris (1992a) notes that such works serve the crucial function of preserving history, correcting misconceptions, and offering nonmainstream interpretations of events. But she recommends that students' attention also be called to the positive experiences shared by people of color, such as stories showing the close ties of family and community. These works may grow from everyday life rather than from extraordinary or dramatic events. For example, in *Tar Beach* by Faith Ringgold (1991), a young girl dreams of flying through the sky with her baby brother to see significant places in the city.

Benefits of Multicultural Literature

Harris notes that students gain the same cognitive benefits from reading multicultural literature as they do from reading and discussing any excellent works. Involvement with multicultural literature can improve students' comprehension and vocabulary and expand their background knowledge. Students can become familiar with works and styles that can serve as models for their own writing.

Multicultural literature offers the additional advantage of raising students' consciousness of their own cultures and the cultures of others. Through multicultural literature, students have the chance to explore both the similarities and differences among groups. Multicultural literature may help students, of both mainstream and nonmainstream backgrounds, to become more tolerant and understanding of others. *Too Many Tamales* by Gary Soto (1993) shows customs that might be unfamiliar to many students. Yet this work can help students recognize that all groups have their own customs. As a follow-up activity, students might be asked to prepare illustrations for their own book of family celebrations.

Harris (1992a) considers the situation in which children have a steady diet only of mainstream literature. This situation can be harmful to mainstream students because it limits their view, fails to develop their knowledge and understanding of other cultural perspectives, and does not prepare them to interact with those of other backgrounds. Reading a multicultural work such as *My First American Friend* (Jin, 1990) may give mainstream students insights about the fears and struggles of immigrant students.

Nonmainstream students need to read multicultural literature to get the message that the contributions and experiences of their cultural groups are valued by the school and by society. Through multicultural literature, teachers can give nonmainstream students the message that they have lives and experiences worth writing about. For example, in *Night on Neighborhood Street*, Eloise Greenfield (1991) presents poems of scenes likely to be familiar to students who live in the inner city.

Practical Considerations

Harris (1992a) recommends that classroom teachers make their own decisions about whether to make multicultural literature part of the classroom literacy program. She believes that multicultural literature is likely to have a positive effect only when teachers sincerely want to share these books with their students. Harris does not think teachers should be pressured to use multicultural literature. If teachers are compelled to use this literature before they feel ready to do so, they may convey a negative attitude about the books and the groups portrayed to their students. "Ideally," Harris writes, "teachers should want to include the literature because it is part of world literature, many of the works are excellent, and children deserve to expand their knowledge of the world's cultures and histories" (p. 193).

Multicultural literature presents new challenges, Harris notes, and teachers have to develop strategies for solving the problems that arise because of the controversial issues in some of the works. For example, *Mississippi Bridge*, another of Mildred Taylor's (1990) works, is historically accurate and tells a powerful story. Yet this book depicts acts of violence against African Americans as well as the use of derogatory terms for African Americans. On the one hand, this book gives teachers the opportunity to explore issues of racism with students. On the other hand, some adults might judge this work inappropriate for use with elementary students.

Harris points out that authors writing from an insider's perspective often portray characters' language just as they might speak in vernacular English. Patricia McKissack, for example, follows this approach in *Flossie and the Fox* (1986). Teachers who share this book with students might need to explain to parents why they have chosen to use a text including a non-mainstream variety of English, instead of sticking to texts written entirely in standard English.

Finally, Harris notes that some authors present historical events from viewpoints that contradict those usually evident in textbooks. For example, some Japanese American authors use the term concentration camp rather than internment camp to refer to the imprisonment of their people during World War II.

Harris does not see a ready resolution to the many potential controversies surrounding the use of multicultural literature. Teachers cannot easily reconcile these conflicting views, although they can come to an understanding of their own positions on the issues. Harris highlights debatable issues not to discourage teachers from using multicultural literature but to remind teachers to use these books in an informed manner. Multicultural literature can provide all students with the pleasures of powerful language, an engaging story, and all the joys of reading. Taken a step further, these works offer teachers and students the opportunity to explore issues of critical importance in today's world, in particular, the need for social justice and racial equality. ❋

References

Harris, V. J. (1992a). Multiethnic children's literature. In K. D. Wood & A. Moss (Eds.), *Exploring literature in the classroom: Content and methods* (pp. 169-201). Norwood, MA: Christopher-Gordon.

Harris, V. J. (1992b). Contemporary griots: African-American writers of children's literature. In V. J. Harris (Ed.), *Teaching multicultural literature in grades K-8* (pp. 55-108). Norwood, MA: Christopher-Gordon.

Sims, R. (1982). *Shadow and substance: Afro-American experience in contemporary children's fiction.* Urbana, IL: National Council of Teachers of English.

Resources

Day, F. A. (1994). *Multicultural voices in contemporary literature: A resource for teachers.* Portsmouth, NH: Heinemann. Presents information on nearly 40 authors of multicultural literature, including biographies, photographs, descriptions of key works, and classroom suggestions.

Harris, V. J. (Ed.). (1992). *Teaching multicultural literature in grades K-8.* Norwood, MA: Christopher-Gordon. A definitive edited volume, describing the political context for multicultural literature and criteria for literature selection, and featuring chapters on African American, Asian Pacific American, Native American, Puerto Rican, Mexican American, and Caribbean children's literature.

Lindgren, M. V. (1991). *The multicolored mirror: Cultural substance in literature for children and young adults.* Fort Atkinson, WI: Highsmith. Includes chapters by authors Elizabeth Fitzgerald Howard and Walter Dean Myers, as well as an annotated bibliography of 101 recommended books.

Children's Books Cited

Greenfield, E. (1991). *Night on Neighborhood Street.* New York, NY: Dial.

Jin, S. (1990). *My first American friend.* Madison, NJ: Raintree Steck-Vaughn.

McKissack, P. (1986). *Flossie and the fox.* New York, NY: Dial.

Ringgold, F. (1991). *Tar beach.* New York, NY: Crown.

Say, A. (1993). *Grandfather's journey.* Boston, MA: Houghton Mifflin.

Taylor, M. (1990). *Mississippi bridge.* New York, NY: Dial.

Taylor, M. (1976). *Roll of thunder, hear my cry.* New York, NY: Dial.

White, E. B. (1952). *Charlotte's web.* New York, NY: Harper.

Thematic Units

Instruction in the readers' workshop often is planned around *thematic units*. With this structure, book selection and study are organized by themes or topics. Single copies of related texts—as opposed to multiple copies of the same text—are used for reading and discussion. The books are sometimes referred to as *text sets*. The purpose of using thematic units is to help students explore concepts and make connections among related texts.

Some units are based on literary themes (e.g., the value of friendship). Some units (e.g., Japan; the ocean environment), are topically related to studies in other subject areas such as social studies and science. Still other units are based on the works of one author (see Author Study in this chapter), allowing students to discover how a writer uses certain literary techniques or handles a particular genre.

Background

Joy Moss (1984, 1990) coined the term *focus unit* to describe an instructional model for teaching literature in elementary classrooms (thematic units and focus units are essentially the same). Her focus units in literature were developed around a central theme, or focus, in order to:

- foster an appreciation of literature,

- develop higher-level thinking skills,

- improve language skills, and

- serve as a starting point for further reading and writing experiences.

Moss described how the process of reading and comparing features or elements of stories furthered students' concept development by helping them discover relationships among ideas and create a structure for those relationships.

Procedure

Schools may have specified themes for each grade level, giving teachers a starting point in planning. Teachers can find more information about themes and planning from professional resources such as those in Figure 3.7. Having selected a theme, the teacher develops objectives for the unit to guide planning, discussion, related activities, and evaluation. Objectives are based on key concepts that are intellectually challenging and worthy of study. For example, one of Mrs. O'Brien's objectives for her kindergarten unit on ocean animals was: to identify ways people help or harm ocean animals and the ocean environment. Second-grade teacher Mr. Jamal's unit on

References

Moss, J. F. (1984). *Focus units in literature: A handbook for elementary school teachers.* Urbana, IL: National Council of Teachers of English.

Moss, J. F. (1990). *Focus on literature: A context for literacy learning.* Katonah, NY: Richard C. Owen Publishers.

Children's Books Cited

Steig, W. (1971). *Amos and Boris.* Scranton, PA: Farrar, Straus, & Giroux.

friendship included as one of his student objectives: to describe how the actions and attitudes of story characters can promote friendship. Ms. DeRego's unit on the works of Jean Craighead George included the following objective for her fourth graders: to understand and give examples of how the author's knowledge of the natural world shaped her writing.

The teacher may elect to read some of the selections aloud, especially for younger students or less-experienced readers. Mr. Jamal decided to begin his friendship unit by reading aloud Aesop's "The Lion and the Mouse" followed by *Amos and Boris* by William Steig (1971). He led discussions about these stories by asking his students about the characters. How were they alike? How were they different? How did the characters feel about each other? How did they show their feelings? What could the author's message be? Students discussed how the characters in each story helped ◆

Figure 3.7   LIST OF RESOURCES FOR THEMATIC UNITS

Resources for Thematic Units

- *Adventuring With Books: A Booklist for Pre-K - Grade 6, Tenth Edition.* J. M. Jensen & N. L. Roser, Eds. Urbana, IL: National Council of Teachers of English, 1993.
  An annotated list of 1,800 titles published between 1988 and 1992, grouped by topic and age level.

- *Collected Perspectives: Choosing and Using Books for the Classroom.* J. Moir, M. Cain, & L. Prosak-Beres. Boston: Christopher-Gordon, 1990.
  An annotated list of 488 titles by genre and age level, including related titles and activities for extending responses.

- *Creating Classrooms for Authors: The Reading-Writing Connection.* J. C. Harste & K. G. Short, with C. Burke. Portsmouth, NH: Heinemann, 1988.
  A good discussion of text sets (pp. 358-365), including book lists for various types of text sets (e.g., story versions, story structures, and different illustrators of the same text).

- *Focus on Literature: A Context for Literacy Learning.* J. G. Moss. Katonah, NY: Richard C. Owens Publishers.
  A companion to Moss's 1984 volume, emphasizing focus units using traditional literature.

- *Focus Units in Literature: A Handbook for Elementary School Teachers.* J. G. Moss. Urbana, IL: National Council of Teachers of English.
  Describes focus units on animals in literature, authors, the world around us, literature around the world, friendship, heroes and heroines, survival tales, and fantastic characters. Includes lesson descriptions and book lists for each unit.

Figure 3.8   A SIXTH-GRADE TEACHER'S NOTE TO THE SCHOOL LIBRARIAN

Maddie,

I'm starting a unit on survival. Will you please reserve copies of the following books for me:

Island of the Blue Dolphins, Scott O'Dell

Julie of the Wolves, Jean Craighead George

Slake's Limbo, Felice Holman

Call It Courage, Armstrong Sperry

Hatchet, Gary Paulsen

These are the titles my students and I know about. Any other suggestions? I'll drop by the library soon. Thanks!

Charlene

---

each other when each one needed help, and how that showed friendship. Later, students read other friendship books independently, choosing from a collection Mr. Jamal assembled that included some of Russell Hoban's stories about Francis and Arnold Lobel's stories about Frog and Toad.

For older students or more able readers, the teacher may give book talks about the selections in the unit and then ask students to choose two books to read independently (see Figure 3.8 for one teacher's ideas). Questions to guide the readings and discussions may be handed out or posted. The teacher may want to read aloud one book as a focus for initial discussions. As students read their selections, further discussions center around their books, with comparisons and contrasts to the book read aloud.

Discussions may be conducted with small groups, the whole class, or even partners. Recording key points on charts, in response journals, or by other means will help students as they work toward the objectives for the unit. New learning should be related to prior knowledge. The teacher may want to have students express and share new insights and information through the visual or dramatic arts as well as by writing.

Teachers may involve their students in developing discussion questions, suggesting follow-up activities, and even selecting books for the unit. Units may be based on expressed interests of students. Students should be asked to evaluate the books, the discussions, and other unit activities as well as their growing understandings of the unit's theme and key concepts. ✳

Author Study

An *author study* is an in-depth examination of multiple works by a single author. Teachers use author studies in the readers' workshop to help students explore the craft of writing and discover how authors communicate with their readers.

Background

Examining authors' works in depth involves looking closely at why authors make certain choices as they develop a piece of writing and how they craft their writing to achieve the effects they want. Rebecca Lukens' (1990) analysis of the elements of fiction (character, plot, theme, setting, point of view, style, and tone) provides a good starting point for considering how and why authors do what they do. In examining story *characters* (people, animals, or sometimes inanimate objects with human qualities), Lukens describes how central characters who are fully developed, those we can see many sides of, are critical to the quality of a story. Readers see these characters as believable and care about what happens to them. Readers also relate to characters who change in realistic ways over the course of the story and are affected by story events. *Plot*—a sequence of events involving story characters and their actions—moves the story forward and engages the reader through the use of conflict, suspense, and a sequence of events. Good plots, like well-developed characters, make us care about the story.

Theme or unifying truth holds the story together and takes it beyond the immediate events into a more universal commentary on society or human nature. Powerful themes help us remember a book long after story events fade. *Setting*—that is, time and place—may be integral to the story or merely a backdrop. Authors can use settings to carry readers to another time and place. Authors use *point of view* to tell readers the story from the perspective of certain characters, coloring what we know and how we view it. *Style* is the way the author uses words to achieve a desired effect. The use of a style that fits the story's characters, setting, and plot makes us believe in the world the author creates. *Tone* tells us how the author feels about the subject, just as tone of voice conveys a speaker's feelings.

Procedure

Author studies can be done by the whole class, a small group of students, or an individual. Teachers often use whole class author studies to introduce authors whose works seem to have the ability to communicate strongly to readers. Author studies also may evolve from a student's (or group of students') love for a book, leading to the exploration of other works by that author.

When selecting an author for study, the teacher looks for someone whose work both she and the students will enjoy and learn from. Some authors write about strong characters readers identify with or may emulate. Some write plots that grab the reader and keep him engrossed in wanting to know what happens next. Others engage readers with powerful themes or a unique style. While authors of fiction are frequently selected for study, many authors of nonfiction are good choices also. Some examples of both are listed in Figure 3.9.

The teacher gathers as many different titles as possible, including multiple copies of some titles so students can read and discuss in small groups or do paired reading. A letter to parents informing them of the planned study may result in students bringing in their own copies of the author's books to share. The teacher also locates background information about the author. Articles in *Something About the Author* (Commire, 1990) give basic biographical data, a complete list of the author's published works, and sometimes interviews and other more detailed information. Publishers often have

Figure 3.9   SUGGESTED AUTHORS FOR AUTHOR STUDY

Fiction Authors	Nonfiction Authors
For lower grades (K - 3):	
Byrd Baylor	Aliki
Eric Carle	Joanna Cole
Tomie de Paola	Gail Gibbons
Eloise Greenfield	Patricia Lauber
Leo Lionni	
Cynthia Rylant	
Allen Say	
William Steig	
John Steptoe	
For upper grades (4 - 6):	
Betsy Byars	Carolyn Arnold
Sid Fleischman	Brent Ashabranner
Jean Craighead George	Isaac Asimov
Scott O'Dell	Russell Freedman
Katherine Patterson	Jean Fritz
Mildred Taylor	Kathryn Lasky
Yoshiko Uchida	Seymour Simon
Lawrence Yep	

photographs and fact sheets about their authors that they will mail out upon request. Videotapes showing authors at work and home are another good source for helping students see the author as a real person (see Resources at the end of this article).

Teachers often share the author's biographical information in one or two mini-lessons, highlighting interesting facts about how the author works or something in the author's background that has contributed to his or her style of writing or choice of content. Mini-lessons should include brief book talks about several of the titles available in the classroom, using them as illustrative examples of the author's style. After that, the teacher may want to give students several sessions to select books and read independently. As with thematic literature units, the teacher may want to read aloud one book as an anchor piece, a book all students will have in common for discussion. For younger students, the teacher may read aloud several of the selections. Some teachers tape record as they read so that students can play the tapes later and follow along in the book.

From these initial experiences, the students and the teacher begin to discuss what they notice about this author that makes her writing unique, interesting, or special in some way, using the literary elements described in the background section as a starting point. The discussions might begin with the whole class and move into small groups as students do more reading and find others who want to talk about the same books they do. With older or more able students who are reading longer books, the teacher may set up a plan in advance, working with the class to decide which titles will be read in common.

The teacher helps students focus on issues such as how the author sets up story conflict, shows characters' growth and change, takes a point of view, develops themes, uses language to convey mood, and other aspects of author's craft. For example, the first graders in Mrs. Shima's class reading Marc Brown's books learned how he included his children's own names in his illustrations and other "fingerprints" in his work (see the example of a classroom bulletin board in Figure 3.10). A group of students in Mr. Jamal's second-grade class reading Byrd Baylor's books noticed her love of the desert and realized how much factual information came through in her poetry. From the background information they read, they learned that Baylor writes about things she likes to do and does a lot of research before writing. When some of Ms. DeRego's students did an author study of Katherine Patterson, they noted and admired the strong characters she created and explored how these characters dealt with major events in their lives.

Follow-up activities give students opportunities to put together their findings in interesting and informative ways. Students have made posters, charts, bulletin board displays, and book jackets. They have given speeches, choral readings, and dramatic performances. They have shared their learning with other classes and visitors to the classroom; they have taken home

Figure 3.10 BULLETIN BOARD: AUTHOR STUDY OF MARC BROWN

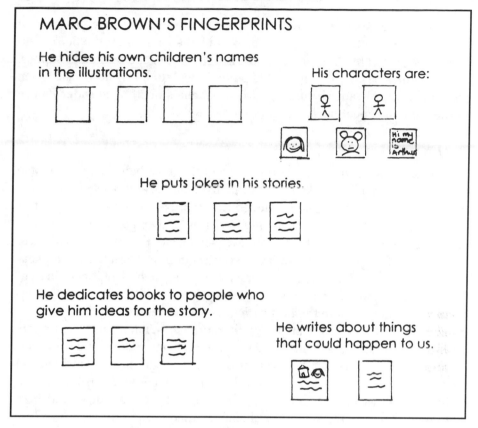

portable items to show parents and other family members. These and other activities provide evidence that students are making connections with authors and that authors are helping them acquire and improve their literacy. ✳

References

Commire, A. D. (1990). *Something about the author: Facts and pictures about contemporary authors and illustrators of books for young people.* Detroit, MI: Gale Research.

Lukens, R. J. (1990). *A critical handbook of children's literature* (4th ed.). New York, NY: HarperCollins Publishers.

Resources

The author studies handbook: Helping students build powerful connections to literature, L. Kotch & L. Zackman, Scholastic, 1995. How-to strategies for using real authors as models for writing and making connections among authors, books, and readers.

Get to know, Harcourt Brace videotape series. A series of videotapes on authors and illustrators designed to help students see the person behind the story.

Genres

All teachers seem to know those students who read only one type of book—science fiction, perhaps, or books about sports, or all the books featuring the character Encyclopedia Brown. While teachers want to support these reading passions, they also hope to widen students' horizons. When planning for the readers' workshop, then, teachers need to consider how to excite students about books of different genres.

Background

A *genre* is a "type of literature in which the members share a common set of characteristics" (Lukens, 1990, p. 13). When Rebecca Lukens wrote this definition, however, she cautioned that there are often as many differences as there are similarities among works in a given genre. Yet she finds genre classifications useful for several reasons. One, they make us aware of the scope of children's literature beyond familiar stories and nursery rhymes. Two, in different genres literary elements such as plot and characterization function differently. Three, using genre classifications help teachers and children explore the rich variety of literature.

The broadest classifications of literature are *fiction* and *nonfiction*. Within fiction, the three main categories are realism, fantasy, and traditional literature. (Figure 3.11 shows a diagram of different genre types.) *Realism*, as the label implies, deals with stories that could happen. Realistic children's stories may have contemporary or historical settings, and they often deal with social issues or problems common to children and adolescents. Historical fiction is a type of realism that has become increasingly popular in classrooms. Teachers find it gives students a vivid sense of life in a particular period in history while immersing them in conflict, suspense, and believable characterizations.

Fantasy employs settings (imaginary worlds), characters (such as animals or plants that speak), and situations (the use of magic to generate events, for example) that are not known to exist. Good fantasies, nevertheless, make their worlds believable. In science fiction (one type of fantasy) for example, scientific laws as we understand them are the foundation for futuristic inventions and scenarios. In *fantasy* stories involving animals that speak, the animals often retain characteristics that fit their species.

Traditional literature encompasses many types of stories passed down from the oral tradition. Variations on the same tales may come from many cultures, attesting to the universality of human needs and desires. Folktales, fables, myths, legends, and epics are common types of traditional literature.

Nonfiction generally is divided into two main categories: biographies and informational books. *Biographies* (and *autobiographies*) give factual accounts of the lives of individuals. *Informational books* tell facts and related concepts about numerous topics in science, social studies, history, etc. Nonfiction books are written in both narrative or expository format.

Procedure

Teachers can introduce students to different genres through mini-lessons, reading aloud, discussions, and book talks. During these activities, teachers will want to talk with students about literary elements (such as character, plot, theme, setting, point of view, style, and tone) and how they are treated in various genres. For example, setting is obviously a more important element in historical fiction or science fiction than it is in most contemporary realistic fiction. Stock characters in traditional tales—the wicked stepmother, the cruel giant—are very different than the multidimensional portraits of characters in most realism and fantasy. Students can explore similarities and differences in genres as they read and talk about books.

A third-grade teacher developed a unit on traditional literature by beginning with myths. She read aloud several creation myths from different cultures and talked with students about what they noticed. She also set up a special book display of myths on other natural phenomena (earthquakes, lightning) for students to browse and borrow from. Students were encouraged to give book talks during whole-class sharing about the titles they had read. From these experiences, the students were able to develop a list of characteristics of myths and begin to understand the genre of traditional literature.

The unit continued with folktale variants. Students were asked to read and compare two or more versions of "Cinderella," the "Gingerbread Boy,"

Figure 3.11   A DIAGRAM OF LITERATURE GENRES

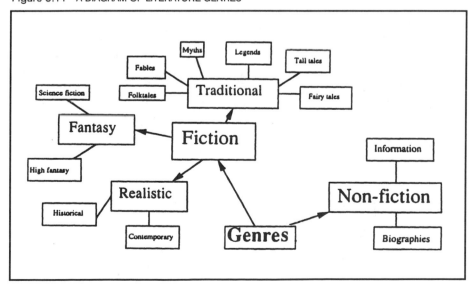

Materials

Selecting books and other materials for the readers' workshop can be one of the most pleasant tasks on a teacher's "to do" list. Here is an opportunity for teachers to collect favorite reading materials and materials for literature responses to share with their students and to impart their enthusiasm and love of reading as they talk about their choices.

Background

The basic materials for a good readers' workshop are high quality literature and other reading matter, not elaborately decorated bulletin boards and classroom displays. Carol Avery (1993) talks about changes she has made in materials selection for her classroom. In her early years of teaching, she chose materials to create an attractive and enticing classroom that "rivaled the fast-paced stimulation of Saturday morning television cartoons" (p. 62). She came to realize, however, that the room was a reflection of her own interests, not those of her students. She noted that although parents and fellow teachers sometimes admired her well-decorated room, no students ever commented on the room's appearance. Now she leaves bulletin boards empty for the children to decorate and concentrates on the essentials: the classroom library, art supplies, props and puppets, games and puzzles, media equipment, and tools for writing.

Procedure

Teachers who value and emphasize reading in their curriculum generally have classroom libraries that house a variety of types of reading materials. Books, of course, are the mainstay of the library, with many types of literature, both fiction and nonfiction, included (see Selecting Literature in this chapter). Books of different genres can be grouped in labeled bins, so that students inspired by reading an interesting legend or an exciting work of science fiction can find other books of the same genre. Books by the same author or on the same topic can be displayed similarly.

Magazines, newspapers, brochures, pamphlets, catalogs, fliers, and other written materials also are important to include in a classroom library. In addition, certain types of maps and posters are designed to be read as well as viewed. It can be a real revelation to students to see the variety of ways print is used by stores, museums, nature centers, theme parks, and other organizations to inform, educate, and entertain people. Including these different formats may even inspire different types of student publications.

Part of the classroom library might include a multimedia center if equipment is available. Books with accompanying audiotapes are popular with some students. A table can be set up with tape players, headsets, and a special display of books and tapes, which are easily kept together in ziplock plastic bags. And of course a world of information is available via computer, both through the Internet and CD-ROMs.

Other worthwhile materials are props students and teachers can use to tell stories or to reenact stories they have heard or read. Puppets, flannel boards with accompanying story characters, and other props can be set up in a storytelling corner or a drama center. Special materials for younger readers include big books; easels for holding large sheets of newsprint with poems, songs, chants, etc. for choral reading and singing; and pointers. Besides their use by teachers, pointers can be used by students to "read the room." In this procedure, students are given pointers and told they can move around the room to read any of the information on charts or other displays. Young children delight in using the pointer to lead a group of classmates in the reading of a favorite poem or chant.

Materials for written or drawn responses to literature include lined, bound response journals (many teachers use composition books), a variety of pencils and colored pens, erasers, highlighters, various types and sizes of lined and unlined paper, staplers, and other art supplies. Painting in response to stories heard or read is an excellent means of expression, especially for younger students. Easels, paints, and large sheets of newsprint can be set up in a special area for this activity.

Teachers use mini-lessons to let students know early in the school year what materials are available in the classroom and what uses they might make out of them. As the year progresses, teachers may need to remind students how to find materials they need and different uses they can make of the materials at hand. Parents may have supplies they would be happy to donate; a request for donations and a list of possibilities can be included in the classroom newsletter. ❋

Reference

Avery, C. (1993). *And with a light touch: Learning about reading, writing, and teaching with first graders.* Portsmouth, NH: Heinemann.

Cross-Curricular Integration

Integrating reading with the teaching of other subjects is a natural link in a balanced literacy program. *Cross-curricular integration* increases opportunities for instruction and learning by connecting the readers' workshop to other subject areas. It enables students to view information from different angles, integrating ideas developed from a literary viewpoint with content knowledge in order to enrich both perspectives. In addition, it provides more class time for reading, writing, thinking, and exploring new information.

Background

Teaching reading skills during a social studies lesson or using a science trade book for a reading lesson is not a new idea. Teachers' ever more tightly-packed schedules demand that class time be used as skillfully as possible to cover as many objectives as can be managed by the teacher and students. However, true cross-curricular integration goes beyond the need to maximize learning time. At its best, integration enables students to do work that is meaningful and worth the expenditure of time.

Constance Weaver (1994) describes a process of growth teachers experience as they move toward giving students greater responsibility for their learning. Teachers typically begin by developing *theme units*, which Weaver defines as "meaningful, teacher-directed activities on a topic of study" (p. 430). A more complex type of theme study is *theme exploration*, where a "broad teacher-chosen topic initiates subsequent student choices" (p. 430). Students determine what related topics or issues are meaningful to them and pursue their individual interests. The most open model is the *theme cycle*, in which "students and teacher together determine topics and questions to pursue" (p. 430). In theme cycles, new topics grow out of previous explorations; teachers and students collaborate in creating units of study.

Procedures

Moving toward student-centered instruction for cross-curricular integration is a gradual development for most teachers. A good first step is to work on thematic units during the literature portion of the readers' workshop (see Thematic Units in this chapter). From there, teachers can branch out to the use of trade books in their content area lessons, relying on fiction as well as nonfiction to help students learn concepts through a variety of experiences. For example, Ms. DeRego read aloud *A River Ran Wild* by Lynn Cherry (1992) to her fourth graders to introduce a science/social studies unit on water pollution. This beautifully illustrated trade book tells of the restoration of the Nashua River in New Hampshire. After students listened to and discussed the information in the story, they began making a list of topics they might want to explore related to water pollution. In this case, the teacher limited the overall theme; she was not ready to have students move into air pollution, noise pollution, or other related subjects since she had no resources to share with them. She did have a good collection of trade books (put together with the help of the school librarian) on oceans, streams, rivers, lakes, wetlands, and how practices from factories, other businesses, communities, and individuals have led to water pollution. Students formed groups of three or four based on the specific topic they wanted to research. They read trade books on their topic, read the section on water pollution in their science textbook, found related information on communities in several social studies textbooks, took notes, talked together, and planned how they would share the information they learned with the whole class. Several groups chose to make posters, one group wrote and performed a short dramatic presentation, another group wrote a letter to the local newspaper, and another group dressed up as different types of pollutants and explained their role in causing damage to rivers and streams.

The next time the teacher does this cross-curricular unit, she could expand to theme exploration by beginning with a broader theme (e.g., ecology) and allowing students' research to branch off into a wider range of related topics, such as endangered animals (including studies of individual endangered species such as whales, cheetahs, pandas, etc.), ecosystems such as the Florida Everglades and Hawaii's rain forests, or natural and human-made disasters and their effects on people and the environment. Authors known for their writings on nature and ecology topics (e.g., Jean Craighead George, Gary Paulsen, Patricia Lauber, Seymour Simon) can be introduced. The periodical *Book Links* is an excellent resource for finding fiction and nonfiction books that relate to topics and themes in a variety of content areas (address and phone number listed in Resources at the end of this article). The *Once Upon a GEMS Guide* (GEMS stands for Great Explorations in Math and Science) is another resource for linking literature with content studies. The goals for the unit usually can be covered regardless of the specific direction students' interests take. The teacher reviews these goals with the class so students can consider them in choosing their particular topics. Students can be taught to use the K-W-L strategy (which stands for what I Know, what I Want to Learn, what I Learned) to help them organize their research questions and findings (see cross-curricular integration in Chapter 7 and Figure 7.12.

Teachers who want to develop cross-curricular theme cycles with their students can begin by explaining the grade level requirements for their school and asking students what additional topics they want to study. Sometimes grade level requirements can be enlarged to include students' suggestions, and sometimes the students' interests are broader and the requirements can fit under them. Teachers who do theme cycles strive to develop fewer, broader themes (e.g., interdependence, diversity, transitions) under which many topics will fit. Goals for student learning tend to focus more on skills, strategies, habits, attitudes, and values to be developed, as opposed to specific content to be acquired. As students explore topics within an initial theme, they often come across information that leads them to new areas of interest for a later theme cycle. ✳

Reference

Weaver, C. (1994). *Reading process and practice: From socio-psycholinguistics to whole language, second edition.* Portsmouth, NH: Heinemann.

Resources

- *Book Links*, 434 W. Downer Place, Aurora, IL 60506-9936, (708) 892-7465.
- *The Complete Guide to Thematic Units: Creating the Integrated Curriculum* by A. M. Meinbach, L. Rothlein, & A. D. Fredericks, Christopher-Gordon, 1995.
- *Once Upon a GEMS Guide* and other GEMS materials can be ordered through Lawrence Hall of Science, University of California, Berkeley, CA 94720, (510) 642-7771.
- *Theme Immersion: Inquiry-Based Curriculum in Elementary and Middle Schools* by M. Manning, G. Manning, & R. Long, Heinemann, 1994.

Children's Book Cited

Cherry, L. (1992). *A river ran wild.* Orlando, FL: Harcourt Brace, Jovanovich.

Connections to the Home and Community

Reading experiences are enhanced when students see themselves as members of a community of readers that includes their families and other important people in their lives. Teachers can structure the readers' workshop to include ample opportunities for students to make these connections.

Background

Research shows that parent involvement has a positive effect on student achievement. Au, Mason, & Scheu (1995) examined classrooms where teachers built connections with families and communities. They noted two areas where teachers worked to strengthen parent involvement: communication with parents and enlisting parent participation in children's literacy activities. Communication with parents included many types of written communication (letters, notes, newsletters), conferences, and open houses. Enlisting parent participation included activities parents could do outside of school, such as reading aloud to their children and taking them to the public library, and activities within school, such as volunteering to be readers, listeners as children read to them, and presenters of information or special activities. Other family members were welcomed also, since some parents were not able to participate in the classroom.

Procedure

Before the school year starts, the teacher will want to begin building connections between the school and the home. Some teachers mail letters to incoming students and their parents, others telephone to talk, and still others pay personal visits to as many homes as possible. This early communication is used to let students and families know that the teacher is interested in them and their lives beyond the classroom. The teacher tries to learn more about his students—special interests and talents, special challenges they face in their lives, the family structure. The teacher also may describe his plans for the upcoming school year, discuss his beliefs about teaching and learning, invite parents and other family members to support classroom efforts in whatever ways they can, and ask for their ideas on strengthening the connections. Some teachers ask parents to complete a questionnaire telling about their child's reading habits and attitudes, interests, and any other information parents feel the teacher should know in order to help their child learn best. Figures 3.13 and 3.14 give a sample of a teacher's letter to parents and of one parent's response.

Once school starts, regular communication can be accomplished efficiently through monthly newsletters. Students can participate in helping to determine what goes into each newsletter, and older students can be responsible for much of the content and layout. Computers, if available, make this

Figure 3.13 BEGINNING-OF-YEAR LETTER FROM TEACHER TO PARENTS

Dear Parents,

I have enjoyed getting acquainted with your child during these past two days. We have begun to settle into the school routine and come together as a classroom community.

In order to help me work more productively with your child, I would appreciate your responses to the following questions. Please take some time to respond and send this sheet back on Monday if possible.

Sincerely,

Student's name _____

Parent's name _____

1. What would you like me to know about your child?

2. How does your child spend time on his/her own at home?

3. What are your goals/expectations for your child this year?

Figure 3.14 ONE PARENT'S RESPONSE TO THE TEACHER'S BEGINNING-OF-YEAR LETTER

August 23, 1996

Dear Parents,

I have enjoyed getting acquainted with your child during these past two days. We have begun to settle into the school routine and come together as a classroom community.

In order to help me work more productively with your child, I would appreciate your responses to the following questions. Please take some time to respond and send this sheet back on Monday if possible.

Sincerely,

Judy Scheu

Judy Scheu

Student's name _Billy Penaroza_ Parent's name _Susan & Bill Penaroza_

1. What would you like me to know about your child?

    Billy is very athletic (started surfing at 5yrs.), and I know he's going to excel in sports. This type of enthusiasm spills over to all aspects of his life. He's very motivated about school

2. How does your child spend time on his/her own at home?

    We've moved into a new home, so of course he's mostly interested in going out and playing with the new friends in the neighborhood - friends are very important to him. He loves nature and exploring, things that make you think

3. What are your goals/expectations for your child this year?

    Billy's very happy inside, and though I don't wish to be a demanding parent, I find it very easy to just expect of Billy continued happiness, and success in reading, growth, and learning about the world.

an easier task. Newsletters are a good place for teachers to communicate the themes, authors, genres, etc. being studied that month and to ask parents for support. For example, when the class studies Native American tribes in their area, parents could be asked if they have books on this topic, titles to recommend, or any artifacts they could share. Families could be asked if any members have special knowledge they would be willing to share with the students.

Another vehicle for communication is a journal that circulates between the student, teacher, and parent. Some teachers write weekly to each child's parent, some write to half the families one week and half the next, and some write to each student on a similar schedule. In these classes, students write weekly to their parents also, telling them of school happenings and personal news. Parents are encouraged to respond to their child and to the teacher in the same journal, creating a record of positive events and special memories, a place to share concerns that anyone (parent, teacher, or student) has, and a place for dialogue in everyone's busy schedules.

In addition to keeping up with what the class is learning, parents need to know how their own child is progressing. Involving parents more fully in the assessment and evaluation process is discussed in Connections to the Home and Community in Chapter 11.

Within the classroom, parents (or other family members) as volunteers can be a valuable resource. Parents who are avid readers may enjoy reading aloud to the whole class, small groups of children, or individuals. They can also serve as listeners for students needing extra support as they read, such as beginning readers, second-language learners, and students with special needs. When students do follow-up projects for the books they are reading (e.g., dramatic productions, art activities, writing), parent volunteers can help organize and monitor some of the groups as the teacher works with others.

Parents also are wonderful resources for information. In a typical class, students' parents hold jobs in a variety of fields and have different interests and areas of expertise. Inviting parents to talk about their work or their interests, especially as these activities relate to an area of study going on in the classroom, can add an important new dimension. More importantly, parent participation helps students see how people in the community are a part of their learning environment.

Connections to the school community can be promoted through activities such as the Great American Read Aloud Day, where adults nationwide are asked to take time to read to children. A first-grade teacher asked several staff members to visit her classroom that day to read to her students. One visitor was the physical education teacher, who read from several books: *The Gym Teacher From the Black Lagoon* (Thaler, 1994), a book given to him by his fellow teachers on a special occasion; a nutrition book he was reading to help him keep up with changes to the health and nutrition field; and a truck repair manual his son and he consulted regularly in the repair and maintenance of the family truck. ✳

Reference

Au, K. H., Mason, J. M., & Scheu, J. A. (1995). *Literacy instruction for today.* New York, NY: HarperCollins College Publishers.

Children's Book Cited

Thaler, M. (1994). *The gym teacher from the black lagoon.* Jefferson City, MO: Scholastic.

favorite books along with introducing new ones. Particularly with less able readers, hearing books read aloud helps them keep up with the information and ideas their peers are getting from reading independently. Older students and more capable readers benefit just as much from being read to, but their teachers may have less time to devote to this activity due to the increased demands of teaching specific content areas. If so, these teachers may use reading aloud as an enticement to expose their students to the wide range of good literature available, perhaps reading selected chapters of a longer book and providing several copies for students to borrow and finish independently, or reading short stories, poetry, or folk tales.

Teachers usually begin the year with exciting, humorous, or other highly engaging books that seem to fit the needs and interests of their students. For example, a first-grade teacher read aloud *Noisy Nora* (Wells, 1973) to her lively class early in the school year. After their first field trip, she read *The Day Jimmy's Boa Ate the Wash* (Noble, 1980), a comical story of Jimmy's pet boa constrictor coming along on a class field trip. A fourth-grade teacher whose class was made up of students from two different campuses started the year by reading aloud *Be a Perfect Person in Just Three Days* (Manes, 1984), a humorous look at a young boy's attempts to fit in and be accepted. As the year progresses, teachers report being able to read more thought-provoking works because students have become attuned to listening carefully and critically to stories, and to thinking about themes, characterization, complexities of plot, style, and other story elements. The same fourth-grade teacher read aloud *Bridge to Terabithia* (Paterson, 1987) part way through the school year; her students enjoyed this sophisticated book about friendship and death.

Reading aloud is a skill that improves with practice. Teachers may want to rehearse with the selection they have chosen, particularly if the text is long or complex. Changing voice tones to represent different characters, varying speed to match story action, pausing at dramatic moments, reading smoothly through intricate sentence structures, and taking time to show illustrations will enhance the story for the listener.

Reading aloud fits well with other parts of the readers' workshop. Thematic units, author studies, and genre studies can all be introduced with the teacher reading aloud one of the books in the collection chosen for study. In all these cases, the book read aloud serves as the anchor piece, a common denominator students can refer to and use as a basis for comparison with other works (by the same author, on the same theme, or in the same genre).

Reading aloud has another benefit. A student may want to join a particular literature discussion group because she wants to read the book selected by the group, even though it is beyond her reading capabilities. For a student who has good listening comprehension, the teacher may be able to arrange for a reader—an adult volunteer, for example. Thus, a less able reader can participate in more sophisticated literature discussions and increase her experience with literature that challenges her thinking.

An excellent resource for choosing good literature to read aloud is Trelease's *The Read-Aloud Handbook* (1989). Carol Avery's...*And With a Light Touch* (1993) contains lists of suggested books for reading aloud that were compiled with the help of her first graders. Perhaps the best source of recommendations comes from fellow teachers and from students themselves.

✳

References

Anderson, R. C., Hiebert, E. H., Scott, J. A., & Wilkinson, A. G. (1985). *Becoming a nation of readers: The report of the Commission on Reading.* Champaign-Urbana, IL: Center for the Study of Reading.

Avery, C. (1993). Chapter 16: Suggestions for reading aloud to children. In ...*And with a light touch.* Portsmouth, NH: Heinemann.

Children's Books Cited

Manes, S. (1984). *Be a perfect person in just three days.* New York, NY: Bantam.

Noble, T. H. (1980). *The day Jimmy's boa ate the wash.* New York, NY: Dial.

Paterson, K. (1987). *Bridge to Terabithia.* New York, NY: Harper.

Trelease, J. (1989). *The new read-aloud handbook.* New York, NY: Penguin Books.

Wells, R. (1973). *Noisy Nora.* New York, NY: Scholastic.

not know strategies for book selection, this topic should be addressed in an early mini-lesson. If students do not have favorite authors, introducing them to good authors should be another group of mini-lessons. Two or three authors whose works have some connection could be introduced, compared, and contrasted during a single mini-lesson. Other mini-lessons can be devoted to specific authors whose books the teacher feels every student in the class should know and read.

For older students who receive grades, the grading system for the readers' workshop should be a topic explained fairly early in the school year. For all students, discussing the evaluation system is important. Even very young students need to know the teacher's long-range expectations. How students' own goals fit into the evaluation system is also a good mini-lesson topic.

Deciding on other mini-lesson topics as the year progresses requires an ongoing assessment of students' immediate and long-term needs. For example, fourth-grade teacher Chris Tanioka noticed that many of her students responded to literature in a static way, looking at their reading from the same angle each time they wrote. She began her next mini-lesson by putting up an overhead of an article she had read in a research journal. She explained how researchers had looked at the written responses of fifth and sixth graders and noticed four different types of responses (writing down what you visualized as you read, putting yourself in the character's shoes, responding in another form such as poetry, and making connections to your own life). As she described each one, she read an example of a student's response from the article. Then she said, "See if you can use one or two of these ideas when you write in your response logs this morning." Later, during whole-class sharing, one boy read part of his response to a chapter from *On My Honor* (Bauer, 1986): "I could feel my stomach muscles rise in fright. How could Tony drown so quick? Why didn't he yell or something?" This student was able to apply the mini-lesson by putting himself in the place of one of the characters (Carroll, Wilson, & Au, 1996).

Mini-lessons can be effective with small groups or individuals. For example, as the teacher leads a literature discussion, he may note that one or more students are having difficulty with some of the story vocabulary. He might decide to take a few minutes to review the use of multiple cue systems for decoding and finding the meaning of unfamiliar words. Or he may feel that the discussion is not being greatly hampered and decide to conduct a mini-lesson with the individual or group at a different time to address this need. Skill lessons are more efficiently handled this way, with students forming flexible skill groups as needed and not being assigned to a remedial group on a permanent basis.

Many teachers keep a list of the mini-lessons they have taught as a resource for future years. Even with a personalized list though, teachers will find themselves making changes in response to the differing needs of each successive class. This balance of planning and flexibility is what makes mini-lessons a powerful teaching tool. ✳

References

Atwell, N. (1987). *In the middle: Writing, reading, and learning with adolescents.* Portsmouth, NH: Boynton/Cook.

Carroll, J. H., Wilson, R. A., & Au, K. H. (1996). Explicit instruction in the context of the readers' and writers' workshop. In E. McIntyre & M. Pressley (Eds.), *Balanced instruction: Strategies and skills in whole language* (pp. 39-63). Norwood, MA: Christopher-Gordon.

Children's Book Cited

Bauer, M. D. (1986). *On my honor.* New York, NY: Dell.

Clay's work on information systems provides a useful, practical framework for thinking about issues of word identification. Thinking at first in terms of the three cue systems helps teachers to keep their teaching focused on helping children to gain independence as readers, moving forward from their present reading behavior. In contrast, focusing on a lengthy list of skills may cause instruction to be diverted to issues that do not relate to children's immediate needs as readers of continuous text. ✳

References

Clay, M. M. (1991). *Becoming literate: The construction of inner control.* Portsmouth, NH: Heinemann.

Clay, M. M. (1993a). *Reading recovery: A guidebook for teachers in training.* Portsmouth, NH: Heinemann.

Clay, M. M. (1993b). *An observation survey of early literacy achievement.* Portsmouth, NH: Heinemann.

Children's Book Cited

Womersley, J. (1996). *Carlos.* Boston, MA: Houghton Mifflin Early Success.

Masking

The children in Ms. Johnson's kindergarten class had just finished reading a familiar big book, *Meanies* by Joy Cowley (1990) during the readers' workshop. They enjoyed reading about how meanies slept in garbage cans, drank bath water, and ate old bubble gum.

Ms. Johnson got out a cardboard mask and used it to frame a word. "Take a close look. Can you tell me what this word is?" she asked. The children identified the word as *meanies*.

"Tell me what you notice about the word *meanies*," Ms. Johnson continued. The children made observations, noting that the word began with an *m*.

"Like my name," Michelle added. Robin pointed out that *mother* began with the same letter as *meanies*.

The children named the other letters in the word: *e, a, n, i, e, s*. "Two *e*'s," commented Letisha. Ms. Johnson praised the children for their observations. She asked them to help her start a list of words that all started with the letter *m*, like *meanies, Michelle*, and *mother*. The children suggested other words, including *Mark, monster*, and *milk*. Ms. Johnson wrote the words on a sheet of chart paper. She told the children they would continue over the coming weeks to add other words that began with m. Following this procedure with a number of big books, Ms. Johnson was able to teach her kindergarten students all the initial consonant sounds, developing their knowledge of what Clay (see article in this chapter) calls the visual cue system.

On another occasion Ms. Johnson put the cardboard mask around the word *mean* in the sentence, *Meanies all do mean things*. She asked the children to identify this word and to tell what they noticed about it. The children noticed that they could turn mean into meanies by adding the letters *i, e,* and *s*.

Calling Attention to Words

As this example shows, *masking* is a way of calling children's attention to the words within a text and to the letters that make up those words. When used during the shared reading of big books, it can be an effective approach for developing children's knowledge of phonics and other decoding skills. Masking, like other word identification activities, should be used after children have had the chance to enjoy a big book on a number of occasions and have become thoroughly familiar with the text.

Holdaway (1979) discusses three different forms of masking. The first, seen in the example with Ms. Johnson's class, involves a simple cardboard mask or frame. In this case the mask is used to isolate the target word so that it is easy for children to focus on it. The mask may also be used to isolate a phrase or sentence, rather than just a single word.

As this examples shows, the teacher's beginning goal for vocabulary development is to help students become aware of new and interesting words and phrases. This goal is accomplished by developing lessons based on vocabulary and language drawn from literature. The new vocabulary is written on charts that remain posted on the wall, and new examples are continually added.

Look In, Look Around

At the third grade and above, teachers continue to promote interest in new words. In addition, they teach students strategies for deriving the meanings of new words as they read. One approach to teaching students to get a sense of what a word means is called *look in, look around* (Herman & Weaver, 1988). The example is based on *Mufaro's Beautiful Daughters* by John Steptoe (1987). First, the teacher has the students read the literature, following an appropriate method. Students are given slips of paper and asked to make a note of any new or interesting words or phrases encountered while reading the story. In *Mufaro's Beautiful Daughters*, students might note the word *transfixed* in the sentence, "She stood transfixed at her first sight of the city."

The teacher tells the students that she will be teaching them how to figure out what a word might mean by doing two things: looking around the word, and then looking in it. The strategy can be represented visually for students, as shown in the chart in Figure 4.7. The teacher explains that looking around the word means thinking about what is happening in that part of the story. It also means looking at the sentence in which the word is found.

Figure 4.7   LOOK IN, LOOK AROUND CHART

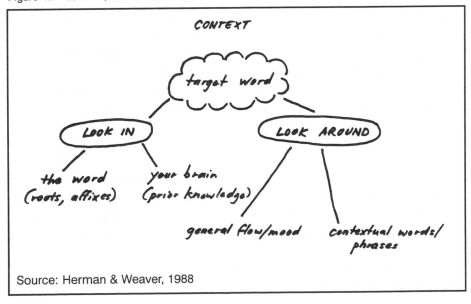

Source: Herman & Weaver, 1988

In having students look around the passage, the teacher elicits from students that Nyasha and her father had left their village to see the king. In having students look around the sentence, the teacher guides them to notice that the word has something to do with how Nyasha felt when she first saw the city.

After she has shown the students how to look around the word, the teacher explains how to look in the word. This process involves analyzing the word itself: seeing if it is a compound word, checking for familiar words or word parts, and looking for the base word and affixes. In the case of *transfixed,* the students might spot the base word *fix* and the *ed* ending. Some might recognize the common syllable *trans,* which appears in words such as *transportation.* The teacher guides the students to make inferences about what *transfixed* might mean, reminding them that the word tells something about how Nyasha felt when she first saw the city. Students might infer that someone who is fixed in one place does not move, and that in this case Nyasha might be surprised, amazed, or stunned by her first glimpse of the city.

The teacher concludes the lesson by telling the students that they can use the look in, look around approach whenever they want to know something about the meaning of a new word. Follow-up lessons on the look in, look around approach might be conducted at least once a week until the teacher is confident that students have an understanding of the approach and are able to apply it when reading.

The look in, look around approach is consistent with the idea that people do not have dictionary-style definitions of words in their minds. Instead, they have a general sense of what a word means. A person's knowledge of what a word means is built up gradually, through encountering the word in a number of different contexts, perhaps through hearing someone speak or watching television, but usually while reading (Nagy, Herman, & Anderson, 1985). Of course, teachers will still want to teach students how to use a dictionary, but with the understanding that people learn the meanings of most words through wide reading over time, not through memorizing dictionary definitions.

Extending the Approach

In addition to teaching students to apply the look in, look around approach to books assigned during the readers' workshop, the teacher should teach students to use the approach when they are reading content area textbooks or articles. Lessons proceed in exactly the same manner. The application to content area reading is perhaps even more important than to the reading of narrative text. This is because content area texts in the upper elementary grades and above, such as science and social studies texts, often introduce a great deal of new vocabulary. Students must learn this new vocabulary in order to understand the key concepts.

- Did you have strong feelings throughout the story? What did the author do to make you feel strongly?

- What is the idea behind the story that gives point to the whole? (What do you think the author wanted you to learn from the story? What is the author's message?)

- Is this story, though different in content, like any other story you have read or watched in its form and structure? (Does this story remind you of any other story? Why? How is it the same? How is it different?)

Teachers can show students how stories are similarly constructed using a story matrix. In this matrix, elements common to all stories are listed across the top line, and information from each story can be entered underneath. This is particularly effective for genre studies, author studies, and thematic units, where students can examine similarities in characters, settings, story problems, events, solutions, and themes (see Figure 4.9 for an example). In addition, the matrix can show students how story elements are organized, helping them become familiar with story structure.

As students learn to examine the form and structure of stories they read, they discover ideas for their own writing. Analyzing how and why characters change, and what make the changes believable, can greatly improve children's own stories, which otherwise may have one-dimensional characters who do things with little apparent motive. Looking at how plots are driven both by external events and by characters' internal reactions and motivations can help students create more believable and imaginative plots when they write. Examining authors' use of language can provide students with excellent examples for their own poetry and prose. ✳

References

Au, K. H., Mason, J. M, & Scheu, J. A. (1995). *Literacy instruction for today.* New York, NY: HarperCollins College Publishers.

Sloan, G. D. (1991). *The child as critic: Teaching literature in elementary and middle schools* (3rd ed.). New York, NY: Teachers College Press.

Written Responses to Literature

During the readers' workshop, students write in response to the literature they are reading (Routman, 1991; Parsons, 1990). The main purpose of having students engage in written response is to give them the chance to express their individual thoughts and feelings. Often, these responses are personal reactions to the literature, and the content of each student's written response is unique (see Rosenblatt, Chapter 2). Many teachers have students do their writing in tablets referred to as literature response logs.

Responses in a First-Grade Class

Teachers often find that students come to the classroom with their own preferred ways of responding to literature. For example, a first-grade teacher asked her students to bring a favorite book from home to share on the first day of school. The children brought a variety of books, including picture books, informational books, and poetry books. The children talked about their books, telling the title, author, and why the book was special to them. Then the teacher asked the children to write or draw about their books. She suggested that they consider why they had selected that particular book to share and what made it a favorite.

Later, the teacher reviewed the children's written or drawn responses. She found that their responses fell into four categories. Most focused on why they liked the book (for example, "I liked this book because it's about friendship") or on a favorite part (for example, "The part that I thought was funny was the man going into the hat shop and trying the hat on but it was too big"). A few told what the story was about. For example, one student wrote:

> The story was about a mother who had a baby. She sang him a song
> and rocked him. When he grew the baby grabbed his mother's watch
> and flushed it down the toilet. When the boy was sleeping his mother
> would creep into the room and sing.

Two students made connections between the books and their own lives (for example, "The reason I brang the book is because when I grow up I am going to be a scientist and study sharks"). The children's initial written responses provided the teacher with an opportunity to assess their comprehension, appreciation of literature, and writing skills.

Because the teacher wanted to extend the children's approaches to written responses, she taught a mini-lesson focused on ways to write responses to literature. Referring to specific examples, the teacher discussed the four kinds of responses the children had made: what they liked about the book, their favorite part, what the book was about, and connections to their own lives. She helped the children classify their responses and began a chart

Figure 4.10   FORMAT FOR LITERATURE RESPONSE LOG ENTRIES

Summary 📖	Personal Response ♡	Think Questions ?	Vocabulary - Page # and New Word
- Main idea	- Like or don't like	- Why?	- Look In
- Beginning Middle End	- Agree or don't agree	- How?	- Look Around
	- Favorite part or favorite character	- What would happen if?	- Look It Up
- Characters Setting Problem Solution	- Prediction	- I wonder . . .	
	- Connection to life		Language
- Important events or information	- Compare to another story		- Awesome adjectives
			- Vivid verbs
			- Precise nouns
	Message		- "Show not tell"
Author's and how use it	I can in my life		- Similes
			- Other "powerful language"

Source: Pat Nakanishi, 1996 (Reprinted with permission of Pat Nakanishi)

class in a discussion of the strengths shown in these responses.

Mrs. Nakanishi taught the students to write personal responses and think questions as the basis for future literature group discussions. When she introduced the students to think questions, she emphasized that these questions should be about something the students really wanted to know. The answer to these questions should not have been given in the chapters the students had read so far.

In the second stage, Mrs. Nakanishi taught the students to engage in paired or partner reading (see Paired Reading, Chapter 5). Although the students read in pairs and could discuss their responses, they were responsible for writing individually in their thinking journals. When the students began to share their written responses in literature discussion groups, Mrs. Nakanishi taught them to evaluate their performance in these groups. Each student was asked to:

- participate
- listen
- be positive

In the third stage, Mrs. Nakanishi had the students read chapters of the novel independently and continue to prepare their own written responses. This stage brought the students closer to her goal of developing independent, lifelong readers. As the year progressed, students began to depart from the four-part format for written responses, choosing to use their own formats instead. Often, the four parts were still present in the responses, but students had blended them together in their own ways. Like the first- and second-grade teachers, Mrs. Nakanishi used students' written responses to literature as a means of assessing their reading comprehension.

These examples show how students across the grades can be taught to write in response to literature. Written responses play an important part in the readers' workshop. They serve the purposes of allowing students to respond individually to the literature, preparing students to participate in literature discussion groups, and providing teachers with evidence to assess students' ability to understand and appreciate literature. ❋

References

Parsons, L. (1990). *Response journals*. Portsmouth, NH: Heinemann.

Routman, R. (1991). *Invitations: Changing as teachers and learners K-12*. Portsmouth, NH: Heinemann.

Responding Through Drama and Art

Students may respond to literature in a variety of ways during the readers' workshop. These include discussions in Experience-Text-Relationship lessons (see article in this chapter), teacher-led grand conversations (see Wells and Eeds, this chapter), or in literature discussion groups (see article in Chapter 5), and writing in preparation for these discussions (see Written Responses to Literature, this chapter). Drama and art provide students with other valuable ways of responding to literature and developing comprehension ability.

Creative Drama

Creative drama involves having students act out parts of the literature using gestures, movements, facial expressions, sounds, changes in voice, and so on. Mary Jett-Simpson (1989) argues that creative drama can readily be used both to develop and assess students' comprehension of literature. Creative drama can occur before, during, and after the reading of literature.

Before reading, creative drama can be used to activate background knowledge. *Lon Po Po*, translated and illustrated by Ed Young (1989) is a version of the Red Riding Hood story from China. Before students read this story, the teacher can have them act out the scene in which Red Riding Hood is questioning the wolf. The teacher can ask the students to think about how the story they will be reading, *Lon Po Po*, is similar to or different from the story of Red Riding Hood.

During reading, teachers can guide students to engage in what Jett-Simpson terms *predictive creative drama*. In planning, the teacher selects a key episode to be dramatized. As students read through the story, the teacher guides them to make predictions. After students have read each section of the text, the teacher has them decide whether their predictions were correct or need to be revised. Before students read the key episode, the teacher has them dramatize what they think will happen. In *Lon Po Po*, the teacher can have the students stop reading at the point where Shang, the oldest child, has aked the wolf to tie the rope to the basket. The teacher asks the students to work in small groups to develop a dramatization of what will happen next. After different groups of students have presented their dramatizations, the teacher leads the students in a discussion of similarities and differences in their presentations, and the evidence in the text lending support to each of the predicted outcomes. Jett-Simpson suggests concluding the lesson at this point, leaving the students in suspense. The next day, students read to find out what happened, and they compare the author's decision about the course of the story with their own predictions.

When students have completed the story, creative drama offers an excellent means both of deepening comprehension and of assessing what the students have learned. The teacher leads students to identify episodes in the story. Students make storyboards, series of sketches, showing the episode they will be acting out, and they practice their acting. When the complete dramatization is performed, it can be videotaped.

Readers' Theater

In this approach students create a script from the literature. The script may cover the whole story or perhaps just a scene or two. When performing, the students read the script with expression.

The teacher begins by having students discuss the part of the story that they would like to highlight, and together they review that section of the text. The teacher familiarizes students with the format for creating the script, showing them how the characters' names will be followed by a colon and the words to be spoken by each character. *Lon Po Po* is a relatively easy story for students to convert into a Reader's Theater script, because the text contains a lot of dialogue. The teacher reminds the students that they may wish to change the author's wording, and that they may need to add dialogue of their own.

When the group rehearses its reading of the script, the teacher has the opportunity to promote expressive oral reading. For example, the teacher can have the student playing the part of the wolf lower his voice and speak with a growl. Students can have several rehearsals to practice and improve their performances, before making their presentation.

Art Activities

Instead of asking students for a written response, teachers may ask them to make a sketch reflecting their impressions and understanding of the literature. In *Sketch to Stretch* (Hoyt, 1992), students are given a short time to make a quick sketch to capture their feelings and ideas. The teacher makes a sketch of her own. The students share their sketches, explaining why they chose to present that image. Students gain by seeing the way others choose to display their ideas visually.

Having students draw comic strips can help them understand the sequence of events and cause-effect relationships in a novel. The teacher and students prepare for this activity by bringing in examples of comic strips. The teacher guides students in noticing and discussing the conventions used in comic strips, such as speech balloons and headings. Students can decide upon the episodes they would like to capture in comic strips, and the strips can be published as a comic book retelling of the novel.

To create a movie roll, students decide upon the important scenes in the story. They make a sketch of each scene and then produce a finished product, using paint, colored pens, and other materials. The pictures of each scene are taped together to form a long scroll, with extra pieces of paper between scenes and on each end (see Figure 4.11). The extra pieces of paper on the ends are used to fasten the scroll to two cardboard tubes or wooden handles set in a cardboard box. When the handles are turned, the different scenes can be displayed in the front of the box. Students can show the scenes in their movie to the class, while describing the portion of the story each scene represents.

Dioramas allow students to visualize scenes in three dimensions. Students create scenes within a shoe box or other small box. The inside of the box is first painted to add background effects. Students use a variety of materials, such as clay, cloth, toothpicks, cotton balls, and so on to complete the scene. Dioramas may be left open, so the scenes appear as if on a small theater stage. Or the box may be covered and two holes cut, one for light to enter and one to allow the viewer to peer at the scene.

Of course, drama and art activities may be time-consuming. Au, Mason, and Scheu (1995) note that these activities probably should not be used with every book children read. Furthermore, the time spent on drama, art, and other expressive activities should never be greater than the time originally spent reading and writing about the literature.

Figure 4.11   MAKING A MOVIE ROLL

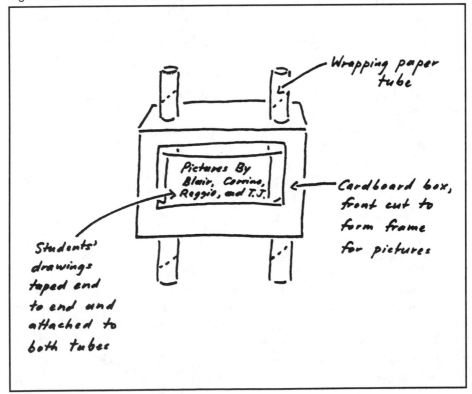

As these examples suggest, drama and art activities can serve the dual purpose of having students reflect upon and express their understandings of literature, and of getting other students interested in these works. Drama and art activities add interest and excitement to the Readers' Workshop. They are not mere extras but valid and enriching approaches for deepening students' appreciation for and understanding of literature. ✳

References

Au, K. H., Mason, J. M., & Scheu, J. A. (1995). *Literacy instruction for today*. New York, NY: HarperCollins College Publishers.

Hoyt, L. (1992). Many ways of knowing: Using drama, oral interactions, and the visual arts to enhance reading comprehension. *The Reading Teacher, 45* (8), 580-584.

Jett-Simpson, M. (1989). Creative drama and story comprehension. In J. W. Stewig, & S. L. Sebesta (Eds.), *Using literature in the elementary classroom* (pp. 91-109). Urbana, IL: National Council of Teachers of English.

Children's Books Cited

Young, E. (1989). *Lon Po Po: A Red-Riding Hood story from China*. New York, NY: Philomel.

Connections to the Home and Community

Teachers who set up their classrooms to involve families and make links with the community know the value of these connections for their students' literacy. As these teachers plan their readers' workshops, they know they and their students can benefit from involving students' families and others from the community in their instructional activities.

Background

Suppose every parent of a child aged one to nine spent 1 hour reading or working on schoolwork with their child 5 days a week. For teachers to spend that same amount of time one-on-one with their students, the cost would equal what taxpayers now pay annually for the entire K-12 public school system (U. S. Dept. of Education, 1994). Therefore, parent involvement effectively doubles the investment in student learning.

We know that parent involvement has a positive effect on student achievement. Studies done on federal education programs (Lyons, Robbins, & Smith, 1983) found observable benefits for students, parents, and staff in programs where parent involvement was high. Positive outcomes included improved student attendance and conduct, improved classroom performance when parents tutored students, active parental support for instructional programs, and an increase in self-confidence and personal satisfaction for parents who participated.

In another study, home factors over which parents have control (such as their child's attendance at school, the amount of television watching permitted, and the variety of reading materials in the home) were shown to account for most of the differences in average student achievement (U. S. Dept. of Education, 1994). Regie Routman states, "Strong parent involvement is not a question of 'Should we?' but rather a question of 'How should we?'" (Routman, 1991, p. 485).

Procedure

Suggestions for involving parents and others from the community as part of the readers' workshop structure have been made in Chapter 3. Here, we look at ways to help parents (and other family members) interested in becoming more actively involved in instruction. Some parents may want to work directly with students in the classroom as teaching aides and classroom tutors. These parents would benefit from a deeper understanding of readers' workshop and how it helps students achieve literacy. For other parents, spending time at their child's school is not an option. Their work schedules, home environment, or language barriers may keep them away from school. Therefore, it is important to help all parents learn good ways of promoting reading at home.

The best ideas are often the basic ones. When parents ask how to help their child be a better reader, teachers can assure them that the most important activities do not require a lot of training. Teachers may want to use part of the class newsletter early in the school year to send home a list of suggestions such as the following:

- Read to your child, every day if possible. Don't stop when he or she gets older.

- Let your child see you reading and know you like reading. Be a good model for literacy.

- Provide books, magazines, and other materials for your child to read.

- Provide a good environment for reading (a quiet, comfortable, inviting spot). If this cannot be done at home, look for alternatives—a relative's or friend's house, the local library, a quiet place at the park.

- Talk with your child about what he or she is reading, and tell your child about what you are reading.

- Make visiting the library a frequent, fun event.

- Encourage your child's reading efforts and praise accomplishments.

- Limit television viewing and encourage reading, writing, listening to story audiotapes, and other literacy activities in its place.

Another important element for parents is knowing what books to read with their child. The teacher can compile a list of suggested readings—perhaps monthly for younger readers and quarterly for older ones—and post it, send it home, or print it in the class newsletter. Students can put together a list of their favorites and distribute it. Teachers can suggest resources such as *The New Read-Aloud Handbook* (Trelease, 1989), and they can send home book order forms from the book clubs for students many publishers have.

Parent workshops can be used to show parents how to support children who are learning through a readers' workshop experience. This can be especially helpful for parents who volunteer as classroom tutors or aides. At the first workshop, the teacher can lead parents through a readers' workshop of their own. Parents select stories to read, read independently or with a partner, write in response to their reading, and form groups to discuss what they read.

At follow-up workshops, parents might learn to give book talks, practice reading aloud, conduct literature discussions to encourage depth and breadth of thinking, and respond to books through writing, drama, and art. Teachers can model book discussions that focus on aesthetic responses, with efferent (content) responses being used to support beliefs, feelings, and reactions to the story.

Workshops, regardless of other content, should address the importance of the parent's role in their child's literacy development. Parents should be praised for their efforts at helping their child. They should be encouraged to continue that support, even as the child gets older and more competent as a reader. Time spent in reading independently tends to drop off dramatically by fourth or fifth grade. Parents need to understand their role in encouraging lifelong reading habits and helping develop positive attitudes about literacy in their children.

For some parents, reading is a difficult activity. They may not be native speakers of English, or they may have had trouble learning when they were in school. Programs such as the Partnership for Family Reading (Handel, 1992) have shown good results in teaching parents to become stronger readers and supporters of literacy with their children. In this program, parents attend a series of workshops, each of which features a high quality children's book, a reading strategy (e.g., making predictions, generating questions, relating the reading to personal experience), practice using the strategy with a partner, group discussion, preparation for reading to children at home, and book borrowing. A program such as this can be a good foundation for strengthening the connections among the school, the home, and the community. ❋

References

Handel, R. D. (1992). The partnership for family reading: Benefits for families and schools. *The Reading Teacher, 46*, 116-126.

Lyons, P., Robbins, A., & Smith, A. (1983). *Involving parents: A handbook for participation in schools.* Ypsilanti, Michigan: High/Scope Press.

Routman, R. (1991). *Invitations: Changing as teachers and learners K-12.* Portsmouth, NH: Heinemann.

Trelease, J. (1989). *The new read-aloud handbook.* New York, NY: Penguin Books.

U. S. Dept. of Education. (1994). *Strong families, strong schools: Building community partnerships for learning.*

Troubleshooting: What About Phonics?

For nearly 50 years, the topic of phonics has been at the heart of controversies in the language arts field. Unquestionably, teachers conducting readers' workshop need to consider the place of phonics in their instruction. The term phonics means different things to different people. To most language arts professionals, phonics refers to the systematic relationships between letters and sounds in the English language. These relationships are termed visual cues and letters/sounds expected by Clay (1993) and graphophonic cues by Goodman (1969). Clearly, knowledge of these systematic relationships is required if children are to become good decoders, as documented in Adams' (1990) review of the literature on beginning reading.

Key Issues

The question is not whether knowledge of letter-sound relationships is important; this knowledge is obviously critically important to children's development as readers. However, there are three widely debated questions with regard to phonics:

- Should phonics instruction be given to all children?
- How should phonics be taught?
- Should phonics be the most important element in the beginning reading curriculum?

All of these questions have great practical importance to teachers.

With regard to the first question, it has been established that not all children require phonics instruction. Durkin (1966) and others have studied children who learned to read before going to school. These children were able to discover for themselves the systematic relationships between letters and sounds in English. Nevertheless, the majority of children, who do not come to school already reading fluently, can probably benefit from instruction in phonics, particularly if skills are taught in meaningful contexts within the readers' workshop and the writers' workshop. In most schools, phonics instruction can begin in kindergarten, when children can be taught initial consonant sounds, and can conclude in second grade. In the second grade and above, instruction shifts from a focus on phonics to strategies for dealing with multisyllabic words and acquiring new vocabulary.

Flexible Skills Groups

Some children will need little instruction in phonics, while others will require a great deal. Because of these differences, although some phonics lessons may be given to the whole class, many phonics lessons will be given to selected children in a *flexible skills group*. These children are grouped

Paired Reading

In *paired reading*, also known as partner reading, two students read books together. Paired reading provides students with both academic and social support for reading and may be used beginning in kindergarten and continuing through the upper grades. The approach is especially useful when texts are too difficult for some students to read on their own, but not so difficult that close teacher guidance is required. Paired reading is a phase in moving students toward independent reading.

Students may engage in paired reading in order to prepare for a teacher-led or student-led discussion (see Experience-Text-Relationship Lessons and The Impact of Wells and Eeds: Grand Conversations, Chapter 4, and Literature Discussion Groups, this chapter). Paired reading may also be used to promote voluntary reading with younger children or struggling readers, who are not yet able to participate in sustained silent reading.

Forming Pairs

Different procedures are used to form the pairs of readers, depending on the purposes for paired reading. If the purpose is to give all students access to the literature, the teacher may match an able reader with a struggling reader. The teacher can ask the able reader either to help the struggling reader decode and understand the text, or to read the text aloud to the struggling reader. If the purpose is to give students practice in decoding text, the teacher may pair students with similar levels of reading ability. In this case, the students will share in the work of reading the text, because one will not find the task much easier than the other. Students may be allowed to choose their own partners, or to change partners, after they have had some experience with paired reading.

Reading the Text

Teachers can discuss with students different ways of reading in pairs. Often, students take turns reading a page or a paragraph of the text, so the reading is evenly divided. If an able reader is paired with a struggling reader, the able reader may read two or three paragraphs, while the struggling reader reads just one.

Students can be asked to help one another during paired reading without giving away the answers. Teachers can teach students to give one another hints about how to figure out an unknown word. Hints can be worded as questions and written on a chart for the students' reference.

- What word might make sense here?
- What is the first letter in the word?

- How is the last part of the word spelled? Do you know any words with the same spelling pattern?
- Can you get any ideas by looking at the picture?

Students can be told that their job during paired reading is to become better readers, and that this is best accomplished by helping their partners figure out the words, not telling them the answers.

Teachers can encourage students to pause occasionally to discuss the text. They can be asked to talk about their feelings about the text, what they understand, and what is puzzling them.

Role Sets

MacGillivray and Hawes (1994) use the term *role sets* for the frameworks that students negotiate during paired reading. In their study of a first-grade classroom, they discovered that the most common role set was coworkers. In this role set, students worked together to choose the book and shared in the reading. In the second role set, fellow artists, students performed for one another, showing how well they could read. The third role set, which seemed to be the most common, was that of teacher/student. The child assuming the role of teacher used many traditional teaching behaviors, such as asking the other child to "repeat after me." In the fourth role set, boss/employee, the child acting as the boss took control and made all the decisions. Fortunately, this role set was only observed with one pair of children.

The findings of MacGillivray and Hawes highlight the importance of discussing with students appropriate ways to work together during paired reading. They suggest that students role play how they can help a partner without upsetting that person, and what they can say to a partner when their feelings get hurt. Teachers might wish to set aside time every so often for a class evaluation of paired reading. During the evaluation, teachers can cite examples of the positive and negative behaviors they have observed, and the class can brainstorm solutions to problems. ✳

Reference

MacGillivray, L., & Hawes, S. (1994). I don't know what I'm doing—they all start with B: First graders negotiate peer reading interactions. *The Reading Teacher, 48* (3), 210-217.

Voluntary and Independent Reading

Voluntary reading is reading that people do on their own, because they want to read. A term formerly used for voluntary reading was recreational reading, denoting the reading that people do in their free time. Voluntary reading differs from independent reading, which is reading students do on their own but not necessarily because they want to. For example, teachers may give students the assignment of reading a textbook chapter independently. Both voluntary and independent reading are important parts of the readers' workshop.

Voluntary reading occurs when people read because they want to enjoy the experience of reading, adopting what Rosenblatt (1978) calls the aesthetic stance (see The Impact of Louise Rosenblatt: Reader Response Theory, Chapter 2). Voluntary reading, an important part of ownership of literacy (see article in this chapter), is a habit that can bring students pleasure throughout their lives. Teachers can do much to encourage voluntary reading, including reading aloud (see Chapter 4), sharing their own literacy with students (see The Impact of Shelley Harwayne: Teachers as Readers, Chapter 4), and giving book talks (see article in this chapter).

Sustained Silent Reading

Sustained silent reading (SSR) is a time when students, the teacher, and anyone else in the room sit quietly to read books of their choice. SSR goes by a number of different names, including "drop everything and read" (DEAR) and "our time to enjoy reading" (OTTER). Teachers should allow time everyday for SSR. SSR may last for only 10 minutes in a first-grade class and for 20 minutes in the upper grades. For capable readers, SSR is a time for independent reading. For children who cannot yet read on their own partner reading may be substituted for SSR [see Hong (1981) for other suggestions]. SSR is not the same as voluntary reading; the teacher has scheduled this event, and students do not have the option of doing anything but reading. However, SSR is a means of encouraging students to develop the habit of daily reading. Because students choose the books they will read, they have the opportunity to develop their own tastes and preferences as readers. SSR is also a means of increasing the amount of reading students do everyday, an important step toward becoming a capable reader (Fielding, Wilson, & Anderson, 1986).

SSR seems to work best in classrooms where students have time to engage in social interactions around their reading (Manning & Manning, 1984). After SSR, teachers may have students discuss their reading with a partner, or volunteers may tell the whole class about their books. As students listen to one another, they can get ideas about books that they might like to read in the future. SSR, when accompanied by social interaction around books, contributes to the building of a community of readers.

Matching Students with Books

Some students are avid readers who know how to find books they will enjoy. However, some students have yet to develop their own tastes as readers. These students need the teacher's help, first to identify books that match their interests, and second to locate these books. Teachers may start by having brief individual conferences with these students, to discover their hobbies and interests. A sample questionnaire is shown in Figure 5.5. Teachers can then recommend specific titles or get ideas from the school librarian.

Most teachers work collaboratively with students to establish rules for SSR. "No talking, no walking" is a common rule. Examples of other rules are that students may get up just once to look for another book, or that they may do paired reading only in a particular corner of the room. In a fifth-grade classroom, SSR occurred right after recess. The rule was that students had to have their books for SSR ready at their desks before they could go out to recess.

Figure 5.5   INTEREST QUESTIONNAIRE

Interest Questionnaire

Name _____   Date _____

1. What are some things you enjoy doing with your family?

2. Do you have any hobbies?

3. What sports or games do you enjoy?

4. Do you take lessons in art, dancing, or music?

5. Are you a member of a club or group, such as a choir or a scout troop?

6. Do you have any pets?

7. If you could take a trip anywhere in the world, where would you go?

8. Is there a famous person you especially admire?

9. What do you think you would like to be when you grow up?

10. Do you have a favorite book? What makes that book your favorite?

11. Is there a certain kind of book you especially enjoy reading? (If necessary, give examples, such as realistic, adventure, mystery, factual books.)

Chapter 6

Overview of the Writers' Workshop

Writers' Workshop in Mrs. Sally O'Brien's Kindergarten Class

Sally O'Brien introduced the writers' workshop on the first day of school. To begin their first workshop, Mrs. O'Brien shared a story she wrote that told how she felt about coming to school that day, and she asked the students to respond to her story. Next, she asked the children to share their own stories. Soon everyone was busy with paper, crayons, and pencils expressing themselves through pictures, scribbles, letters, and an occasional recognizable word. At the end of the workshop Mrs. O'Brien invited the children to share their stories from Author's Chair (see Chapter 9) and their classmates listened and responded. After Melissa shared, Mrs. O'Brien said, "Let's tell Melissa what we thought about her story." To begin other workshops Mrs. O'Brien's mini-lessons (see Chapter 8) have focused on such areas as invented spelling, picture details, and publishing techniques.

Throughout the year, Sally O'Brien has observed and assessed her students growth as writers in a variety of ways. She has also helped them become aware of their own growth. Before the end of September, Mrs. O'Brien placed a "We Can Do" chart on the bulletin board. From time to time the class has talked about specific writing goals, often as a result of mini-lessons, and Mrs. O'Brien has added new goals to the chart. When students consistently meet a goal, they write their names on the chart beside that goal. Now, in May, most of the children plan, draft, edit, and publish their own stories. The process has become familiar and comfortable.

On this day, the children sit together on the floor. Their teacher reads the book, *Watch Out for the Chicken Feet in Your Soup* (dePaola, 1974), and then she asks the children to think how it is like some of the books they have written. The children know a great deal about authors, how they write and what they write, because they have examined and discussed a large number of picture books this year. They talk easily and relate their own family stories to the book during this mini-lesson.

Next, Mrs. O'Brien takes a status of the class (see Figure 12.3). She speaks briefly to each child about what he or she will be doing before the children are dismissed to get their writing folders. Some children will begin new stories, some will continue with a story in progress, some will reread to check their work, and some will be publishing their pieces.

There is a buzz of activity as the children work—they all have an important message to communicate through writing. A developmental range is evident—a few children draw pictures and print random letters, a few children have several pages of traditionally spelled words—but most children use consonants correctly at the beginning and ending, and often in the middle, of words. Many are aware of vowels and experiment with their use.

Children confer with one another as they spontaneously read aloud, question, and provide assistance. They freely use the many resources available in their classroom. Word lists, which they have contributed to and have illustrated, hang from a chart stand. This "dictionary" is well used. They refer to print on wall posters, and books and materials in the library center.

While the children work, Mrs. O'Brien confers with them informally. She provides support for selecting new topics, asks what children plan to do next, and encourages their independence.

Children check their pieces against a chart before publishing.

Are you ready to publish?

   1. Name?

   2. Does it make sense?

   3. Good pictures?

   4. Title?

   5. Date?

This reminder gives children a purpose for rereading their work. One area in the classroom has a variety of materials useful for publishing so that children can select what they need independently.

Children share their publications with their classmates in different ways. There are individual and group authored books in the classroom library, bulletin board displays, and a special Author's Chair where students

Figure 6.1 KINDERGARTEN STUDENT'S WRITING PIECE

sit to read their published pieces. When Melissa sat in this chair to share "My Pet" (see Figure 6.1) her classmates listened attentively to her soft but confident voice, and they responded with enthusiastic comments.

Mrs. O'Brien plans to help Melissa try a variety of sentences in future pieces, and she will include Melissa in a small group mini-lesson on "ing" endings. She also thinks the class could benefit from a lesson to discuss story titles. ❋

Children's Book Cited

dePaola, T. (1974). *Watch out for the chicken feet in your soup.* New York: Simon & Schuster Books for Young Readers.

Writers' Workshop in Ms. Brenda DeRego's Fourth-Grade Class

Ms. DeRego and her class have participated in a regular writer's workshop. Throughout the year they have worked to identify writing topics that are meaningful and special to them. Ms. DeRego's questions to students have been, "Why is that so important to you?" "What is the main thing you want people to know about your grandmother?" A look at the students' publications in the classroom library reveals their personal involvement and concern for audience.

During the second semester, the class engaged in a theme study focused on preservation of the environment. As a part of the study each student chose a topic to research. Ms. DeRego expected the students to report their research in some written form. She helped them build upon the connections between report writing and the familiar process of their personal writing.

Ms. DeRego often spoke of the students "becoming experts" on their topics in the same way they were experts on their personal experiences. They began with K-W-L (see Figure 7.12) on which they listed what they already knew about their topics and what they wanted to find out. Students read, used their K-W-L form to make notes of interesting information they had learned, conferred with one another, asked more questions, and repeated the cycle in their goal to become experts.

Their talk greatly enhanced this stage of the process. During a variety of groupings—large group, small groups, interest groups, informal conversations—the children shared the interesting information they found. Their talk helped to clarify their thinking, allowed for sharing of their developing strategies and skills, and further strengthened the classroom community of learners.

A variety of resources helped students answer their questions and gain additional information. Ms. DeRego's mini-lessons on notetaking supported their work. When the children felt they were "full" of information, they began a draft of their reports. Ms. DeRego guided the students through several mini-lessons to think of how they could organize their information. Some children liked using a category chart to organize the information they found. On their charts they organized their information into categories such as animal's description, family life and reproduction, home/habitat, food and eating habits, interesting facts. They found their charts provided them with logical support for paragraphing their reports.

Children shared their report drafts during large group and peer conferences. They received feedback about what their classmates were learning and what was most interesting about their pieces. The children worked to add facts, and to present their information in ways that would appeal to their audience. After revising, the children checked their own pieces for mechanics, had an editing conference with a classmate, then turned to a class "editor" for help. The children chose a variety of ways to make their information public.

Paul decided to study an endangered animal, the wolf. He wrote his report from the perspective of a wildlife biologist, which added further interest to his piece (see Figure 6.3). When Paul shared his completed report with his classmates, he told them he was planning to write a poem about wolves. ✻

Figure 6.3 FOURTH-GRADE STUDENT'S WRITING PIECE

Paul G.
5-18

I Speak For The Wolves

Hey, hold it. What are you shooting at?" "I'm shooting at that damn wolf who stole one of my favorite chickens," scramed the angry farmer in disgust. Well, you had better listen up because I'm David the worlds most famous, smartest, and best wild life biologist and I speak for the wolves because I an understand what they say. People think of wolves as "big bad wolves." Well, I have news for you and those people, they absolutly never ever kill a human unless there are hunted or cornered. They are at risk all over North America, Russia, and Central Asia. Now they are extinct over most of Western Europe, although still found in some Eastern Europian countries.

It's habitat is mostly mountains and open country. They eat mostly large animals like reindeer, moose, and caribou. Wolves produce or give birth to about 5-9 cubs born 7 weeks after mating, usually spring. The young cubs are sexually mature at 18 months old.

Wolves usually hunt at night, they may have formed this habit to avoid man. The Tasmanian wolf already has become extinct. They are not part of the wolf family, they are part of the pouched family called marsupials. Wolves may become extinct UNLESS people start putting wolves into game reserves and learn that they only attach the sick. They don't attack sheep or cattle or even humans or whatever people say they do. It is more of a possibility that a bear or cougar would attack sheep or cattle and humans than a wolf.

This country's population is finally learning something the Indians and Eskimos have known all along: when wolves prey upon larger game they acually improve the herds. Many people do not know hat wolves will acually hunt for mice and small rodents as well as for big game animals. Wolves are larger and more powerful than a german Shepard witch it resembles. "Oh, and for your information that wolf over there is not the one who took your chicken it's that coyote over there at the edge of the feild that did it." "Oh, thank you" said the stunned, shocked, and impressed farmer.

ommends that teachers try to understand the processes students use as they think, learn, and write. As teachers develop this understanding, they help students gain an awareness of their mental processes. With encouragement, students can take control of their own learning. Then improvement in writing becomes less a matter of the teachers pushing students and more a matter of students moving themselves forward, because they know where they want to go.

Teachers as Learners

To teach writing effectively, Graves suggests, teachers begin by putting themselves in the position of learners. In particular, they are learning about their students as people. This can be accomplished by listening closely to what students say, by trying to see the world through their eyes, and by accompanying them on walks through their neighborhoods. Students soon reveal themselves as multidimensional and knowledgeable of topics with which the teacher may be unfamiliar.

> Jon read his draft about bows and arrows to his fourth-grade class and when he finished, several of his classmates made comments and asked him questions. His teacher raised her hand and he called on her.
> She asked, "Does a forty-pound bow weigh forty pounds?"
> "No," answered Jon. "It takes forty pounds to pull it back. Mine's backstrung. Do you know what that means?"
> "No," confessed Ms. Kinzie.
> "A backstrung bow has more power. A ten-pound backstrung bow has twenty pounds of power." (Hansen & Graves, 1986, p. 807)

In this example, the teacher was comfortable with the fact that Jon knew more about bows than she did. She encouraged him to show his expertise and to teach others through his writing and oral responses. Students, like adults, will write well and at length when they care about the topic and know a great deal about it.

Teachers face the challenge of helping students to see that they have knowledge and experiences worth writing about. Often, students believe that good writing comes only from exciting or unusual events. As Graves (1994) notes, "Writing comes from the events of our daily lives, from what appears at first glance to be trivial" (p. 36). Teachers can help students to become aware of how writing can and should grow from their everyday experiences. Graves points out that this can be accomplished through mini-lessons. For example, in one mini-lesson the teacher might show students how she has written a piece based on an everyday experience. In another mini-lesson, the teacher might show how fiction can grow from everyday situations familiar to students, such as conflicts between siblings.

When students feel confident in writing about a topic, their voice comes through in their writing. Graves writes:

> Voice is the imprint of ourselves on our writing. It is that part of the self that pushes the writing ahead, the dynamo in the process. Take the voice away and the writing collapses of its own weight. There is no writing, just word following word. Voiceless writing is addressed "to whom it may concern." The voice shows how I choose information, organize it, select the words, all in relation to what I want to say and how I want to say it. The reader says, "Someone is here. I know that person. I've been there, too." (p. 81)

Through the work of Graves and other advocates of the process approach to writing, teachers have come to recognize the importance of concepts such as voice and audience for even the youngest writers. These concepts do not remain mysterious but become understandable to students through teachers' demonstrations. For example, to communicate the concept of voice, the teacher can show students two pieces, one written with voice and the other without, and have students discuss the differences between the two.

In the process approach, teachers show respect for students' ideas and writing. However, as Graves points out, they also do a great deal of teaching, often through demonstrations, to provide students with knowledge, strategies, and skills. Through nudges, they see that students make steady progress toward becoming effective writers. ✳

References

Graves, D. (1983). *Writing: Teachers and children at work*. Exeter, NH: Heinemann.

Graves, D. (1994). *A fresh look at writing*. Portsmouth, NH: Heinemann.

Hansen, J., & Graves, D. (1986). Do you know what backstrung means? *The Reading Teacher, 39* (8), 807-812.

Chapter 7

STRUCTURING THE WRITERS' WORKSHOP

Setting Up Your Classroom

Writing, by its nature, is a "messy" task. A well-organized, predictable workshop environment can heighten a writer's productivity. As writers ponder, seek feedback from peers, shuffle and reshuffle text, it is important that they know where to go for ideas, how to gain support from colleagues, and to have the necessary tools at their fingertips.

Background

A teacher's beliefs about writing will determine the classroom's emotional and physical climate. Nancie Atwell (1987) shared seven principles that provided a foundation for the teaching and learning at her school in Boothbay Harbor, Maine.

1. Writers need regular chunks of time.

2. Writers need their own topics.

3. Writers need response.

4. Writers learn mechanics in context.

5. Children need to know adults who write.

6. Writers need to read.

7. Writing teachers need to take responsibility for their knowledge and teaching.

Atwell's list is a good reference point for teachers as they think about the needs of their own unique students and school situations. Regie Routman (1991), considered her teaching experience in Shaker Heights, Ohio, then added two principles to Atwell's:

- Writers need to feel safe to take a risk.

- Writers need a genuine purpose for writing.

These principles can guide teachers as they structure and arrange their own classrooms.

Procedure

Principles such as those suggested by Atwell and Routman suggest an environment that is meaningful, collaborative, and interactive. They imply that students feel ownership for their learning.

Teachers, therefore, will want to organize their classrooms so that children can move around easily and talk with one another as they go about their writing. Teachers usually cluster student desks to form groups of 4 or, if necessary, 5. Some teachers, especially those with large numbers of students, may designate areas along the classroom edges where students can engage in peer conferences without disturbing others. A place where students can comfortably come together as a whole group is very important. An area rug may signal the spot where children will gather in a circle at the beginning and often at the end of writers' workshop. A special chair (see Author's Chair, Chapter 9) is included from which student authors share their writing with classmates.

Some teachers set aside a special area where students can edit their work. This might be two or three desks placed together or a small table with helpful references nearby. Teachers may arrange a place where students can publish their final pieces of writing. These teachers take care to select and organize the publishing materials so that students can work with little adult guidance or supervision.

Teachers also plan ways for students to share their writing throughout the classroom. Bulletin boards and displays of many kinds highlight students' selected writing pieces. Student publications are placed alongside commercially published books in the classroom library. Students' written messages, observational notes, and letters are prominent and testify to their use of writing for genuine purposes. Kindergarten teachers provide paper and pencils for many purposes such as making grocery lists in the housekeeping center and for labeling creations and making signs near the building blocks.

Throughout the school year, teachers conduct mini-lessons to help students learn to work within the environment they have set up. One of the first lessons may be to set the tone for a calm, purposeful workshop by showing children how they will be expected to leave their desks, perhaps one cluster at a time after pushing in their chairs, to sit quietly on the carpet. Other lessons will deal with routines such as the use of writing folders and other materials (see Materials in this chapter), getting ideas for writing, responding to teacher conferences, seeking peer assistance, sharing, and responding to one another's writing.

It is important that students become comfortable with the physical

Figure 7.1 SAMPLE CLASSROOM LAYOUT

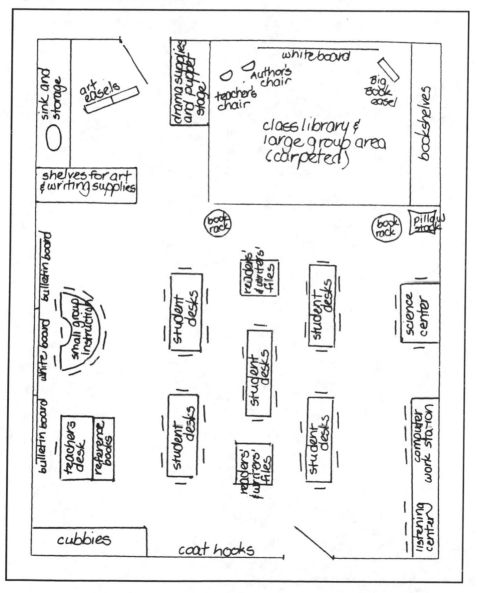

arrangement of their classroom and with the patterns for operating within it. A familiar, predictable environment will support their exploration of the new and unpredictable to be discovered within their writing experiences. ❋

References

Atwell, N. (1987). *In the middle: Writing, reading, and learning with adolescents.* Portsmouth, NH: Heinemann.

Routman, R. (1991). *Invitations: Changing as teachers and learners K-12.* Portsmouth, NH: Heinemann.

Scheduling

Many teachers emphasize that time is one of the most important elements in an effective writers' workshop. Donald and others emphasize that predictable, abundant time is essential if students are to become intensely absorbed in their writing. Teachers will need to examine their schedules and the demands placed upon their instructional time. They may need to do some "creative juggling" in order to present their students with the "luxury" of time to write.

Background

Lucy Calkins (1991) discusses the reasons that predictable, abundant time is so important to young writers. First, if students know that they will be writing tomorrow morning, they can anticipate and plan while they are away from their desks. These students often speak of their experiences, "Last night when me and my family had a flat tire, I thought that would be a good thing to write about today." Students also begin making plans for themselves such as arranging for peer conferences or jotting down notes that they can develop later. Second, Calkins emphasizes that students must have long blocks of time in order to develop and expand their ideas, draft, revise, share—to become completely absorbed with a piece of writing. This need is often contrary to the pace running through many schools due to mounting demands that leave the curriculum fragmented and make interruptions the norm.

Procedure

The ideal classroom schedule would include a one hour-long writers' workshop every day. Many teachers have been able to manage this by thinking more broadly about the curriculum. They know that the writers' workshop encompasses all the language arts so they may find ways to incorporate their curriculum requirements within it. For example, instead of teaching grammar and punctuation as separate subjects, they note the skills their students are to acquire and present them as mini-lessons. Then they support their students' use of those skills as they write. Some teachers bring theme or content unit study into the workshop by taking a month or two during the year when children may write about related topics. This writing often takes the form of research report writing for older students (see Cross-Curricular Integration, Chapter 7 and Classroom Description, Chapter 6). In some classrooms the workshop time is segmented. For example, teachers may include the mini-lesson and time for students to work on writing in one block; sharing takes place at another time later in the day.

There will be teachers who will find it impossible to accommodate the ideal schedule: kindergarten teachers whose students attend school half day,

Figure 7.2

READERS' AND WRITERS' WORKSHOP
SCHEDULE—SECOND GRADE

Figure 7.3

READERS' AND WRITERS' WORKSHOP
SCHEDULE—SIXTH GRADE

<table>
<tr><td>

Readers' Workshop
Writers' Workshop

8:30   Silent or partner reading

8:50   Book sharing (whole class)

9:00   Mini-lesson—Plurals with -es & -ies

9:10   Teacher meets with:

     Henry and Mudge—Mon. & Thurs.

     Arthur's April Fool—Mon. & Thurs.

     Freckle Juice—Tues. & Fri.

     Best Friends—Tues. & Fri.

     Flexible skills groups—Wed.

10:00 Recess

When your group isn't meeting:

• write in your response journals

• keep reading

• work on your book project

• choose something else related to reading

10:30 Read aloud—*Runaway Ralph*

10:50 Mini-lesson—Noticing details

11:00 Independent writing

     Conferences (teacher and peer)

11:30 Sharing

Sign up if you :

• need a conference

• need editing help

• are ready to share (Author's Chair)

</td><td>

Readers' Workshop
Period 3 10:15 a.m.—11:00 a.m.

Mon.—Wed.

Silent reading and response journals—30 min.

Class sharing, book talks—15 min.

Tues.—Thurs.

Mini-lesson & read aloud—15 min.

Literature discussion groups—30 min.

Fri.

Choice time—30 min.

Class sharing, weekly reflection—15 min.

Writers' Workshop
Period 4 11:05 a.m.—11:50 a.m.

Mon.—Wed.

Mini-lesson—10 min.

Writing and conferring—35 min.

Tues.—Thurs.

Writing and conferring—35 min.

Sharing—10 min.

Fri.

Writing and conferring—30 min.

Class sharing, weekly reflection—15 min.

</td></tr>
</table>

upper grades teachers with 45-minute time blocks, teachers who feel that other obligations must be met. They will want to consider how sustained writing time can be allocated for shorter blocks of time. They may plan a workshop that meets three days a week for half a year, or daily for a few months. Fewer, concentrated workshops are of more benefit to students than experiencing writing only once or twice a week. ✳

Reference

Calkins, L. (1991). *The art of teaching writing.* Portsmouth, NH: Heinemann.

ment. We select a form of writing to best suit the purpose of our expression. The forms available to us are many and diverse: lists, diaries, commentaries, reviews, autobiographies, letters, notes, minutes, reports, charts, recipes, brochures, captions, instructions, applications, advertisements, signs, notices, plays, poems, jokes, riddles, menus, editorials, questionnaires, etc.

Whatever terms educators use, they all note that people use a variety of writing forms for real purposes in their daily lives (see Figure 7.6). Therefore, it is important and logical that those forms of expression find authentic purpose within the life of the classroom as well. Writing in which students engage must connect with the curriculum and be addressed to real audiences. Educators also emphasize that teachers must help students understand the characteristics of a form before expecting them to use it effectively. It is a teacher's responsibility to select and share well-written models, guiding students to identify and compare their distinctive elements.

Procedure

During the writers' workshop students choose the form their writing will take. Most frequently they will choose to describe experiences from their lives in the form of reports or personal narratives (memoir). Teachers will want to demonstrate other forms so that students can experiment with a variety of means to express their thoughts and ideas.

For example, letter writing is a form that has many purposes in an elementary classroom. It can be used to share information, persuade, record events, invite a response, find out, inform, and amuse as well as express social courtesies. Children's letter writing frequently begins with note writing, sometimes surreptitiously. Many teachers legitimize this form by placing a container of note paper and a message board in the classroom and encouraging students to communicate with one another. If children need the teacher's attention while he is working with a small instructional group, he may suggest they use notes to communicate with him. Teachers can demonstrate the structure and function of this form by corresponding with students. The Morning Message (see Morning Message, Chapter 8) provides a good model. Teachers can also write personal notes to children to congratulate, thank, and make suggestions. Teachers may use mini-lessons to examine the purposes for which notes are used in the classroom, for example: to request, "Can I use your eraser?"; to apologize, "Sorry I broke your pencil. I thought it was flexible"; to tattle, "Brooke and Cherise are arguing over who's friends with who." As they discuss note writing some children may discover new possibilities to try themselves. Conventions like the importance of signing your name, and choosing words that won't hurt other's feelings are important to this form and might be the subject of other lessons.

Communicating with pen pals provides a meaningful purpose for children's letter writing. Pen pal exchanges may take place within the same school, among schools in the same district, or between classrooms in distant states or countries. Pen pals might be same-age children, older/younger combinations, or even children and adults. Teachers can support children's success with this genre through direct instruction. Primary-grade teachers could use *Arthur's Pen Pal* (Hoban, 1982) to introduce the notion of a pen pal and to discuss the commonalities of this type of letter writing with other familiar forms of communication. Another lesson might focus on the structure of a friendly letter. To reinforce the lesson, a sample letter can be posted to which students can refer as needed. Also, children can learn to construct graphic organizers to plan the content of their letters. They will find that events from their lives can be used to inform, and possibly amuse, their letter-receiving audience. Lessons such as these are applicable to children's friendly letters intended for family members or friends as well as to their thank you and business letters. Teachers' instructional support should help students identify similar characteristics among letters and note differences relevant to the varied purposes and audiences for which they are written.

Letter writing is just one of many forms that teachers will want to offer children. Teachers should decide which forms to introduce and then provide instruction to enhance and support students' efforts. When children have opportunities to explore a wide repertoire of possibilities, they are likely to discover further options and expand their writing experiences. They frequently find ways to imaginatively blend writing forms to create their own unique pieces (see Figure 6.3, a research report written in the style of a personal narrative). ✳

References

Graves, D. (1989a). *Experiment with fiction*. Portsmouth, NH: Heinemann.

Graves, D. (1989b). *Investigate nonfiction*. Portsmouth, NH: Heinemann.

Hoban, L. (1982). *Arthur's pen pal*. Scranton, PA: Harper & Row.

Ministry of Education, Wellington (1992). *Dancing with the pen*. Katonah, NY: Richard C. Owen.

Tompkins, G. E. (1994). *Teaching writing: Balancing process and product* (2nd ed.). New York, NY: Macmillan College Publishing Co.

more skills a list, either general or specific to each individual, can go into their writing folders to check against when editing.

Students need folders to accommodate their writing. Many teachers have students keep two folders, one a working folder (see Figure 7.7) and another for storing completed works. If young children use large-sized paper, they will need large folders as well. Bankers boxes, or specially designed wire holders provide good storage for students' folders at the end of writers' workshop. Assessment portfolios (see Setting Up a Portfolio System, Chapters 11 & 12) are a special kind of folder and teachers need to consider what form they take. Some teachers use regular file folders, some use notebook binders, some like students to design their own.

Students enjoy publishing their stories in different formats throughout the year. A first publication may be the child's final draft stapled into a construction paper cover or a story neatly printed on paper with a special boarder. As the school year continues, students will like to publish books that are cut into different shapes, folded accordion style, or with pop-up features. They will find it interesting to use a variety of art media to illustrate their books such as crayons, markers, watercolors, poster paints, and "findings" to create collages. Wallpaper samples can be glued over cardboard to make attractive book covers. Paper is placed between the book covers and the spine is stitched with dental floss. Students find that special title and dedication pages add a professional touch to their publications.

Other materials contribute to an effective writers' workshop. Rubber stamps and pads allow students to date their writing and mark it "unedited," "revised," or "draft." An overhead projector, transparencies, and markers aid mini-lesson presentations. A typewriter or word processor and printer helps ease the publishing of student writing as does access to a photocopier.

In setting up their classrooms, teachers consider how materials can best be organized to promote student independence, thoughtfulness, and productivity. Open, labeled shelves may house writing materials so that children can access them easily. Teachers usually plan beginning-of-the-year mini-lessons, to focus on managing materials. Young children need to learn how to use the stapler and staple puller. Older students can more easily spot their writing folders in the storage box when each is unique in color or design. If general-use materials are located in various places throughout the room, congestion is eased as students move around to get the supplies they need.

It is a good idea to prepare forms needed for writers' workshop prior to the start of the school year. Frequently, forms are used for status-of-the-class, peer conferences, and editing reminders, to list possible topics and the titles of stories students' have published. ✳

Reference

Lloyd, P. (1987). *How writers write.* Portsmouth, NH: Heinemann.

Figure 7.8   FORMS FOR STUDENTS TO LIST PERSONAL WRITING SKILLS

THINGS I CAN DO WHEN I WRITE

Name _____ Grade _____ Teacher _____

Date   <u>BEFORE WRITING</u>

_____   _____

_____   _____

_____   _____

_____   _____

_____   _____

            <u>WRITING</u>

_____   _____

_____   _____

_____   _____

_____   _____

            <u>REVISING</u>

_____   _____

_____   _____

_____   _____

_____   _____

            <u>EDITING</u>

_____   _____

_____   _____

_____   _____

_____   _____

_____   _____

Figure 7.9   FORMS FOR STUDENTS TO LIST PUBLISHED STORIES

Name _____

Publishing

These are the stories I have published:

Date	Title	Format	Audience	Comments

Figure 7.10   FORMS FOR STUDENT CONFERENCES AND EDITING

GRADE 2 CONFERENCE SHEET

GRADE 2 CONFERENCE SHEET

To _____   Date _____

1.   The part I like is _____

     _____

2.   ☐ characters _____

     ☐ setting   _____

3.   ☐ Tell me more about   _____

4.   ☐ How did you feel when _____

                                        From _____

MY EDITING

Title _____

Author _____

☐   Capitals

☐   Punctuation: . period
                    ? question mark
                    ! exclamation point

☐   Do I need quotation marks (" ") or commas (,)?

☐   Spelling

Cross-Curricular Integration

In a balanced literacy program, students' writing is not limited to the scheduled writers' workshop. Throughout this text we have discussed the role of writing in the readers' workshop. However, writing can serve as a tool across other curriculum areas such as math, science, and social studies. Many teachers have also discovered ways to integrate the content subjects into their writers' workshop.

Background

Gail Tompkins (1994) suggests that writing across the curriculum can benefit elementary students in at least three ways: (1) it encourages learning of content area information; (2) it develops writing fluency, strategies, and skills; and (3) it activates critical thinking skills. Writing contributes to learning because through writing students develop greater knowledge of the subject. When students write in all curriculum areas, they write more easily, and the writing makes their thinking more concrete. As students write they discover, organize, classify, connect, and evaluate information.

Procedures

Many teachers have students use content journals to record information and communicate their learning as they explore a variety of content areas and theme studies. (This is different from personal writing in journals as discussed in Chapter 9.) The journals may be purchased composition tablets or simply paper stapled together between construction paper covers. Students regularly use their journals to review and interpret problems they have solved, and record and reflect upon information discussed or material they have read. Sometimes teachers ask students to use their journals to respond to specific prompts or questions. Open-ended questions such as "What did we do? What did we find out?" will encourage reflection on a math lesson or a science experiment. Students may be asked to use their journals to explain how they worked through and solved a math problem. Before beginning a social studies or health lesson teachers may ask students to do a "quick write" to focus on information they already know about the subject. The teacher may set a timer and for 5 or 10 minutes everyone considers: "What do you know about Bosnia?" prior to a current event discussion or, "What is junk food?" to begin a study of nutrition. Paired with the focus question might be a second question, "What would you like to learn?" At the conclusion of the study students return to their journals to consider "What new things did you learn?" and "What would you still like to know?" Journals provide students with a concrete record of their growth as learners. Students' journal entries give teachers a means to evaluate student learning as well as the effectiveness of their instruction (see Figure 7.11).

Constructing visual organizers such as charts and webs to record information is a valuable strategy for students to develop. Charts can be used to record topic information in an approach developed by Donna Ogle (1986) called K-W-L (see Figure 7.12). The letters stand for the three basic steps in the procedure: assessing what I Know, determining what I Want to know, and recalling what I Learned. Webs can be used to help students record and

Figure 7.11   STUDENT'S SCIENCE JOURNAL ENTRY

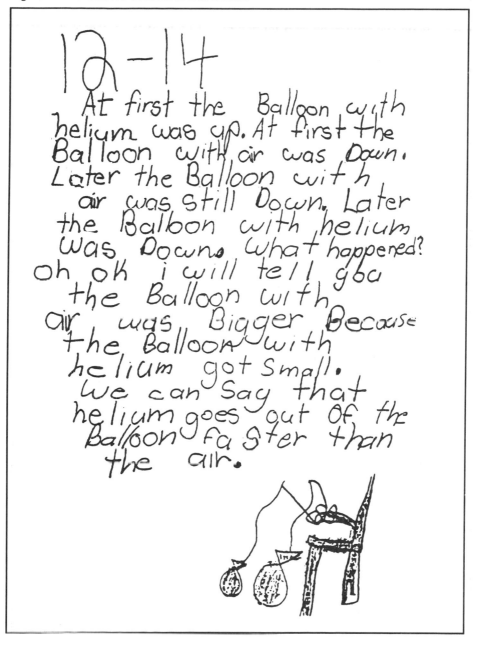

Troubleshooting: What About Pacing?

The curriculum demands of the elementary school are great and growing greater. Teachers frequently begin the school year wondering, "How can I possibly cover all that?" To "get through everything.," many teachers often find themselves racing from one subject to the next pulling their students along behind. They sample broad topics—mammals, drugs, transportation, families and try various forms of writing—poetry, persuasive, fiction, informational report; but they haven't the time to pursue any area in depth. The curriculum is "covered," often concealing more than is revealed.

We know the importance of students' active involvement in learning, but involvement is difficult when students lack time to pursue their interests in depth. It is a struggle for teachers to keep the pace moving so they can "get to everything" and still grant students opportunities to inquire and investigate at length. This issue is as true of the writers' workshop as it is of other subject areas.

Examine Your Curriculum

Lucy Calkins (1994) encourages us to consider our curricula in terms of both depth and breadth. She recommends narrowing our focus within areas of study so that students can probe more deeply and meaningfully. Because schools' curricula are usually presented in broad concepts, teachers often plan their instruction to be broad based. Calkins points out that broad concepts inherently reside within more limited issues and subject areas. She believes we can trust that as students delve deeply into their studies, they will encounter and deal with a broad range of concepts.

Calkins suggests that teachers review their curricula to identify those areas best suited for deep inquiry and those better served by more cursory coverage. Teachers can then schedule longer time segments over several weeks for students to explore some subjects in depth and shorter blocks to focus on more limited curriculum requirements. For example, a first-grade teacher may choose to spend considerable time exploring the role of families, but give just incidental attention to the investigation of holidays. It is important for teachers to make choices about which areas will have greater pay off for student learning and spend more time on those areas.

Within the writers' workshop teachers may want students to experience a range of forms and genres, or the school curriculum may specify the variety to be taught. Some kinds of writing might benefit from in-depth study, others may need only a short amount of attention or be addressed within the longer studies. Teachers need to make choices and set priorities. Knowledge of students and their needs should guide teachers' decision making.

One Teacher's Solution

Jack Wilde (1993), a teacher in Hanover, New Hampshire, provides a model for teacher planning. He paced the variety of experiences offered within his writers' workshop, allotting ample time for students to pursue each one in depth. Wilde explained that there is not sufficient time within the school year to focus on every genre or form in depth. He felt he needed to make some decisions. Based upon his own experiences as a writer, and knowledge of his students, he set goals and made plans. Wilde wanted his students to experience enough variety in the writing forms they worked with to discover at least one with which they were at ease. He hoped that each student could find his or her own voice within a particular genre or form. Wilde acknowledged that a degree of student ownership was lost when he chose to center blocks of the workshop time on specific kinds of writing. Some would argue, he knew, that students should be supported in discovering that voice on their own during free, writing exploration. Wilde learned from experience, however, that with such an open approach opportunities can be lost. Too often people will not risk the unfamiliar. A student may never discover the power of his persuasive voice unless he is expected to write in that form. So, Wilde chose to ask his students to try specific genres and forms to learn what they might offer them. As students explored, he provided help and support, choices, and challenges.

Wilde selected five specific kinds of writing on which to focus: personal narrative, fiction, poetry, persuasive, and informational. Over the course of the school year, each type of writing was studied during the writers' workshop. Several weeks were devoted to each study for example, four weeks for poetry, ten weeks for the informational report. Students were expected to publish a piece of each of the five types after having taken it through the writing process. As students were immersed in their writing, Wilde offered a variety of specific mini-lessons to support their efforts. Because all students were focused on the same type of writing, Wilde's lessons could be more precise and students' support for one another was more focused.

As students shaped their pieces, they explored many broad concepts. They examined character motivation in their fiction pieces and rhyme, rhythm, and word choice in their poetry. Other concepts cut across their work—leads and endings, embedding information, metaphors, flashbacks. They made choices about their topics and ways to express their ideas. Wilde encouraged students to present their informational pieces in a variety of forms or genres such as interviews, diaries, stories, scripts.

Wilde's approach shows that it is possible to "cover" the curriculum and still give students opportunities to engage in meaningful, in-depth exploration. If pacing is an issue, Wilde presents a good model to consider. Teachers will do well to examine their goals and curricula, decide how goals

After his students are settled at their desks, the teacher would likely speak briefly about Groundhog's Day perhaps making connections with news reports they had heard or read before school that morning. The teacher might choose to focus on paragraphing and ask why he had written his message in two paragraphs. He might also review the use of parentheses and ask that students take note of any they discover during times of independent reading.

Teachers who make written messages a part of the school day speak of how much their students value their communications. They also speak of how valuable the messages are in terms of instruction. Daily messages provide a means for teachers to model their own literacy as well as to reinforce skills within a meaningful context. ✳

Reference

Crowell, D. C., Kawakami, A. J., & Wong, J. L. (1986). Emerging literacy: Reading-writing experiences in a kindergarten classroom. *The Reading Teacher, 40* (2).

Mini-Lessons

Mini-lessons are the key instructional component of the writers' workshop. Whole-class mini-lessons usually begin the workshop and are 5 to 10 minutes in length. Small-group and individual lessons may occur throughout the workshop. The focus of mini-lessons may be on workshop procedures, literary concepts (author's craft), or writing skills and strategies (Atwell, 1987). The topics of mini-lessons can be determined by teacher observation of student need, curriculum guidelines, or by student request (see Author Study, Chapter 7).

Background

Lucy Calkins (1986) first introduced the idea of mini-lessons. She compared mini-lessons with "well-timed tips from experts (p. 167)." It is when people are deeply involved in a project or topic that they value and benefit from the instruction of someone more knowledgeable. This is applicable, as well, to children involved in a writers' workshop. It is because they are deeply involved in their writing that lessons aimed at helping them improve are meaningful.

Calkins pointed out that the purpose of a mini-lesson is to "add information to the class pot (p. 170)." Seldom does a lesson call for all children to practice the concept immediately. Perhaps a small number of students will have use for the information at the time it is presented, but it is out there in the classroom. For some students it may resurface in their minds when they need it; other students will have it recirculated for them as classmates talk about the concept during conferences and sharing sessions.

Procedure

It is helpful to use Atwell's ideas for categorizing mini-lessons (see Figure 8.2). To introduce the writers' workshop, a teacher's first mini-lesson will likely deal with the strategy of topic selection (see Selecting Literature, Chapter 7 and Topic Selection, Chapter 8). An important purpose for this lesson is to help students understand that writers think about, or rehearse, their writing prior to sitting down at their desk. Another purpose is for students to understand that the best writing comes from things we have experienced and know well (see Selecting Literature, Chapter 7). Students should see that the ordinary things in life can be viewed and related with interest and freshness. Teachers will explain the importance of these ideas to writers. They will share how they go about choosing writing topics using their own writing as an example. Then they will have students use information from the lesson, perhaps by jotting down some topic ideas and sharing them with a partner. Next, students will select a topic and begin writing.

Topic Selection

Writers write best about topics they know and care about. All people have ideas, interests, memories, and concerns. Teachers should help students identify things that are significant in their lives and support students' exploration of those topics within the writers' workshop.

Background

Donald Graves (1994) is firm. It is a teacher's role to show students how to select topics from the ordinary events in their lives and expand them into a variety of writing forms. Children need guidance and support to find significance within ordinary subjects, otherwise their writing will likely be broad brush "all abouts," focused on big events like a trip to Disneyland, or a retelling of someone else's movie or television drama.

Graves suggests that teachers regularly demonstrate how writing topics are chosen by sharing their own thinking during mini-lessons. The lessons will help children learn of the possibilities for writing within one's experiences.

Teachers can also expect students to verbalize their own topic selection process. Students should anticipate that a teacher conference will include questions such as, "What is your piece about? How did you choose this topic to write about? What will you do with this piece? Who might you share it with?" and be prepared to respond.

Graves points out that students who can count on a regular writing time, and who know they are in charge of the content, will discover ideas for writing throughout the day. When they think, "I could write about that!", rehearsal is often integrated into the process. Rehearsal may take the form of daydreams, sketches, notes, lists of words or diagrams, and conversations as students reflect on their subjects—or a thought (e.g., "The kids will really like this story.") If teachers assign topics they limit opportunities for children to practice the important skills of both choice and rehearsal.

Procedure

Teachers often begin a first writers' workshop with a mini-lesson to show how they might select topics for writing. They brainstorm in front of their students a list of topics they could write about—setting up a new aquarium, decorating a cake for a friend's birthday, concern for a sick aunt, shopping with a daughter. They share briefly and descriptively about each topic explaining that these are ordinary things, but things they know and care about. Then they ask the children, "What are some things you could write about?" As the children share, the teachers ask questions to help students consider their subjects in more detail. "What did you do at the beach? How did you make the sand castle?" Teachers find that after lessons like this, children can choose a topic and begin writing. As children draft, teachers will talk with them individually about their choices. Teachers have found, too, that one lesson is not enough. Mini-lessons concerning topic generation need to continue throughout the year as do their individual, topic-related conferences.

As children become more confident and fluent, teachers will want to help them bring greater focus to their writing. To support students, a teacher will again plan mini-lessons using her own writing to show how she limits her focus to one aspect of an experience. The teacher would begin by showing children how she does this herself by brainstorming a list of subtopics within a larger topic. For example:

> Shopping with my daughter:
>
> * going to the mall
>
> * our conversation in the car
>
> * finding a place to park
>
> * choosing a T-shirt
>
> * lunch
>
>   —which restaurant?
>
>   —our funny waiter
>
> * my sore feet

She would explain that she didn't tell about her shopping trip from beginning to end, instead she limited the story to her daughter's difficulty in selecting just the right T-shirt. Lessons like this will help children learn that when writers focus their topics it is possible to include more description and detail and stories become more interesting. Next, the teacher would ask students to brainstorm a list of subtopics within a larger topic either as members of the large group or as a part of a small group. Later children could try the strategy independently.

It is also effective to plan mini-lessons in which children share their sources of topics. They can be asked to tell where and when they thought of the idea. What did they do to remember the idea? Some students find it helpful to keep a notebook (see Notebooks, Chapter 9) for jotting down story ideas. Some keep paper and pencil beside their beds. As children share ideas about topic selection they soon begin to "borrow" topics from one another. They may also be nudged to think about writing at times and in ways they might not have discovered on their own.

Sometimes teachers use mini-lessons to deal with problematic issues concerning topic selection. Occasionally there is a child who cannot think of anything to write about. Suggesting strategies such as looking around the room or out the window of the classroom—or writing over and over "I cannot think of anything to write"—will usually spark an idea. There are some children whose writing simply retells someone else's story—a video or television show. Teachers need to help them understand that this is inappropriate unless it carries some personal significance. Other children need help in seeing that writing about a future event such as "What I will do at my friends birthday party" is unlikely to produce a good story. Writers usually have many more interesting things to say about events they have experienced than those they are anticipating. Another common issue is the child who continues to write about the same topic again and again. The teacher needs to reflect on why the child may be doing this. Is it safe? Is it a means to grow and improve his writing? Children need to know that improvement in their writing should be apparent over time. It is reasonable to ask how their writing within that topic has improved. It is also reasonable to say, "It's time to switch to a new topic. Do you need my help in doing so?" (see Troubleshooting: What About Struggling Writers?, Chapter 9). ✳

Reference

Graves, D. H. (1994) *A fresh look at writing*. Portsmouth, NH: Heinemann.

Spelling Strategies

What do you do when you don't know how to spell a word? Your response most likely revealed at least one of your spelling strategies. Spelling skills are important in the writers' workshop. As teachers, we must help our students develop a repertoire of strategies in order for them to become independent, competent spellers.

Background

In the past the common strategies suggested to children for spelling unknown words were "Ask the teacher" and "Look it up in a dictionary." With the process approach to writing came an understanding of invented spelling as an appropriate strategy for first draft writing. But then what? What strategies can students use during the editing process? Are there different strategies for beginning, developing, and mature spellers?

Teachers need to help their students address the question, "What do I do when I don't know how to spell a word?" by offering strategies they can use independently. Sandra Wilde (1992) suggests that teachers focus their instruction on five major spelling strategies that she terms:

- placeholder spelling

- human resource use

- textual resource use

- generation, monitoring, and revision

- ownership

Some of these strategies are more sophisticated than others, but none of them are ever completely abandoned by adults. All writers will find occasions for employing each of the strategies.

Procedure

The strategies Wilde proposes provide useful guidance to teachers' work with writing and spelling. The ways in which they approach the specific strategies will depend upon their students' age and development. When teachers talk with elementary-age students, they may want to use the terms we suggest here to make Wilde's ideas more accessible.

Writers use the strategy of temporary *(placeholder)* spelling in order to get their ideas down quickly before they forget. They put down just enough of the word so that they will recognize it later, knowing they are not spelling the word correctly (perhaps not even close to correct). This is the least sophisticated of all the strategies, but one that can be helpful for good spellers as well. Teachers of older children might use a mini-lesson to

Figure 8.3   HAVE-A-GO SHEET FOR SPELLING

HAVE-A-GO

	"Does it look right?"	"Does it look right to you?"	
COPY WORD	FIRST TRY	SECOND TRY WITH A FRIEND	STANDARD SPELLING

Vocabulary Development

The purpose of vocabulary development activities in the writers' workshop is to enable students to use more precise and memorable language in their own writing. Often, students give few details and use the same words over and over again in their writing. The events in their lives are described in superficial terms such as "good" or "fun," while their friends and relatives are "nice."

Vocabulary development lessons center on examples of distinctive language in works of children's literature. These lessons resemble vocabulary development activities during the Readers' Workshop in having the initial purpose of making students aware of interesting words and phrases in literature. They differ in having the additional purpose of helping students to incorporate interesting words and phrases in their own writing.

Collecting New Words

Collecting new words, an approach appropriate for all grades, is shown in this example, based on *Miss Nelson is Missing!* by Harry Allard (1977). The teacher begins by reading the story aloud to the children. When the students discuss the story, the teacher notes the topics of particular interest to them. In this case, the students are likely to be fascinated by one of the characters, Miss Viola Swamp. The teacher has the students make a web of memorable words and phrases related to the topic of interest. For example, students make a web with the words and phrases the author used to describe Miss Viola Swamp: *unpleasant voice, real witch, wicked.* The students may also add words of their own: *mean, cruel, ugly.* The teacher completes the lesson by asking the students to be looking for words that might be added to the list in the future. She reminds them that they may come across such words when they read new books. Later, when students suggest new words, the teacher adds them to the chart. Periodically, the Collecting New Words lesson is repeated with other books. Children can also be invited to make their own lists or webs of vocabulary words.

Author's Craft Lessons

Students need to be reminded that good writing is not just a matter of substituting an uncommon word, such as *humongous,* for a common one, such as *big.* Teachers may conduct lessons to show students how an author uses language to create specific effects. For example, in *Encounter* Jane Yolen (1992) describes Columbus's landfall in the New World from the perspective of a Taino boy. Students can learn from this text how the effective use of vocabulary goes beyond using uncommon words. Yolen describes the

stand the value of invented spelling and of allowing students to maintain ownership of their writing. This basic understanding is usually gained through the kinds of opportunities described above. To help volunteers learn the specific activities they will perform, teachers usually plan instructional workshops or informal training sessions. The teacher will begin by modeling the activity for the volunteers, next the volunteers will practice while the teacher coaches, and then the volunteers practice on their own. If the volunteers' involvement will be to publish young children's stories using a word processor, the workshops can be planned around steps such as these.

(1) The child reads her story aloud to the adult.

(2) The adult asks questions for clarification.

(3) The adult helps the child consider how the story is organized leaving any suggestions for changes up to the child.

(4) The child reads aloud from her draft as the adult types.

(5) As the adult types, volunteer and child make decisions about writing conventions, page breaks, etc.

(6) Two copies of the story pages are printed, one for the child to illustrate and make into a book, the other to be stapled with the draft and filed in the child's writing folder.

Teachers often extend students' participation in literate communities by having them work with students in other classrooms. Teachers of older and younger children often pair up and plan collaborative activities for their students. Usually this time is scheduled and all children participate with a "buddy" from the other classroom. Sometimes "buddies" are older children who provide younger children with assistance in reading and writing. Sometimes the interactions between "buddies" is informal—perhaps letters "mailed" to each other's classrooms or dialogue journals that are exchanged.

These interactions are most productive when children understand the reasons for the activities and how they should be approached. If fifth graders are to effectively guide first-grade writers, they need to know the kinds of support to offer (Morrice & Simmons, 1991). The older students will find it informative to visit the first-grade workshop to observe the students and teacher. The first-grade teacher should allow time to talk with the fifth graders and answer their questions. Each time the "buddies" work together, teachers should help them evaluate the session and make plans for their next session.

Sometimes teachers in two grade levels plan cross-curricular studies for students to investigate together. Often this is a science or social studies topic that is related to a theme unit explored at each grade level. Children use content journals to pose questions, record observations, make notes, etc.

Their informal writing then leads to published pieces collaboratively prepared by the cross-grade level "buddies" and shared with the whole group. Before beginning the study, teachers explain the overall goals as well as the students' roles and responsibilities. After each session children and teachers consider what went well and what needed working on. Then they set new goals. When teachers take care to develop a shared vision, they can expect that student learning will be strengthened. ✳

References

Baker, E. C. (1994). Writing and reading in a first-grade writers' workshop: A parent's perspective. *The Reading Teacher, 47* (5), 372-377.

Morrice, C., & Simmons, M. (1991). Beyond reading buddies: A whole language cross-age program. *The Reading Teacher, 44* (8), 572-577.

Routman, R. (1991). *Invitations: Changing as teachers and learners K-12.* Portsmouth, NH: Heinemann.

dents learn from repeated experience about the conventions of writing. Finally, journals provide students with a means of evaluating their own progress as writers. When students go back through their journals and compare their first entries to the ones they have made recently, they become aware of their growth as writers. Some students will even find their journals valuable in the years ahead, as reminders of their lives at a younger age. ✳

References

Peyton, J. K., & Reed, L. (1990). *Dialogue journal writing with nonnative English speakers: A handbook for teachers.* Alexandria, VA: Teachers of English to Speakers of Other Languages.

Routman, R. (1991). *Invitations: Changing as teachers and learners K-12.* Portsmouth, NH: Heinemann.

Peer Conferences

In peer conferences, students meet with other students to get responses to their writing and ideas about how to improve their writing. Peer conferences benefit student authors because, if they need help with their writing, they do not have to wait until the teacher is available. They also receive a wider range of responses than if their only conferences were with a teacher. Peers who conduct conferences benefit because they gain insights into the writing process and develop the social skills needed to communicate effectively and assist others.

Of course, most students do not automatically know how to help another writer. They need to learn from their teachers how to conduct conferences with peers (Graves, 1983). Many teachers demonstrate conferring skills by conducting conferences with small groups rather than with individual students. Small group conferences give students the opportunity to observe how the teacher helps others improve their writing, for example, by listening attentively, making notes, and phrasing questions and suggestions in a certain way.

Teachers also use mini-lessons to teach conferring skills. For example, the teacher may use one of her own pieces of writing as the basis for a mini-lesson. After stating her own concerns about the piece and reading it aloud, the teacher invites students to make positive comments about the piece and offer suggestions for revision. Later mini-lessons may be centered on similar class revision conferences, but in response to pieces written by student volunteers.

Peer Conferences in Primary Grades

In kindergarten, first, and second grade, teachers often find it helpful to teach children exactly what to do and say in conferences. The recommended procedures and questions are posted on chart paper, providing children with a script to follow. The teacher designs questions to address goals she has for improving the children's writing. As children gain experience with conferences, they can respond spontaneously and will not need to refer to the chart.

In a first-grade classroom, most children were producing drafts of only two or three sentences. The teacher believed the children were ready to develop their ideas into stories, and she taught a mini-lesson showing how stories usually have a beginning, middle, and an end. She encouraged students to extend their writing so that their pieces would have these three parts. To guide children during peer conferences, the teacher wrote the following on a sheet of chart paper:

Things to ask

        Does the story have a beginning?

        Does the story have a middle?

        Does the story have an ending?

Figure 9.4 PARENT LETTER

Dear Parents:

To encourage students to write at home, I'm introducing writing backpacks. These back-packs will be filled with the supplies your child needs to write and publish a simple book at home.

Beginning in October, your child will be bringing a writing backpack home once a month. If there is a certain day of the week that you prefer to have the backpack come home, please let me know by completing the form below.

When the backpack comes home, please take a few minutes to help your child think of a topic of interest and write and illustrate a simple book. There is no one right way of prepar-ing the book. The important thing is that the writing experience be enjoyable for you and your child!

Please remind your child to put all the supplies back in the backpack and bring it back to school the next day. If your child would like to share the book you made together in class, please send the book along, too.

I hope you have fun with our new writing backpacks!

Sincerely yours,

Beth Parker

- -

I would like the writing backpack to come home on the following day of the week:

_____

_____

Parent's name

Figure 9.5 PARENT SUGGESTIONS

Suggestions for Parents

1. Have your child write his/her first draft on the unlined paper. Feel free to make sugges-tions. This draft can be messy!

2. Make the pages of the book by folding or cutting the unlined paper in half. Punch holes so you can use string or yarn to tie the pages together.

3. If you want to use other materials that you have at home, please feel free to do so. For example, you and your child might think of a way to make an interesting cover for the book.

4. Last year, parents came up with all kinds of ideas. In some families, each person did a page of the book. Go ahead and try new approaches!

5. Have fun!

on their own. Most of the children brought their books to school to be shared. In short, writing backpacks seem to be an effective means of fostering students' writing at home with their families. ✳

References

Reutzel, D. R., & Fawson, P. C. (1990). Traveling tales: Connecting parents and children through writing. *The Reading Teacher, 44* (3), 222-227.

Troubleshooting: What About Struggling Writers?

Most students flourish in the environment of the writers' workshop (Graves, 1983). However, teachers often find that there are a few students who struggle with writing. These students are supported through the structures of the writers' workshop, such as a regular time for writing, established classroom routines for writing, and teacher and peer conferences. These features are discussed in Chapters 7 and 8. The importance of keeping these students motivated and involved in the writers' workshop cannot be over emphasized. As shown in the following examples, teachers need to provide additional support for struggling writers within the context of the writer's workshop.

Finding a Topic

One reason children struggle with writing is that they cannot decide what to write about. These students often lack self-esteem, which leads them to believe that their lives are uninteresting in comparison to the lives of others. Melissa, a third grader, was an example of such a student. She did not seem able to identify a suitable topic. Day after day, she told her teacher, Mrs. Loew, that she just didn't know what to write about. Mrs. Loew had already demonstrated to the class how she identified topics (see Topic Selection, Chapter 8), and now she held a writing conference with Melissa in which she asked her to talk about her life. Mrs. Loew soon learned that Melissa perceived her life as very uninteresting. She felt bored in school, and she professed to having no hobbies or interests outside of school. An only child, Melissa spent most of her time at her grandparents' home, because her mother worked at night as a nurse. As Melissa spoke, Mrs. Loew made notes. Then she had Melissa start a list of topics. She asked Melissa to write down these possibilities:

1. Staying at my grandparents' house

2. My mom's job as a nurse

Neither of these topics sparked Melissa's interest, and over the next few days Mrs. Loew continued to offer Melissa strategies for finding a topic. She had Melissa try the following:

- Confer with a friend, to find out what that person was writing about. Mrs. Loew suggested that Melissa might like to write about something similar.

- Write about everything noticed in the room and outside the window (Routman, 1991). Mrs. Loew had Melissa sit at her desk and write down her observations in the hope that an idea would be triggered.

- Think of a special memory, such as a family vacation or a birthday, and try to recall everything about that event (Routman, 1991).

Mrs. Loew remained patient but persistent, letting Melissa know that she expected her to continue searching for a topic. Finally, Melissa approached Mrs. Loew with a draft. She had written about going to visit the hospital where her mother worked. In her conference with Melissa, Mrs. Loew learned that her mother had recently returned to work. Melissa missed having her mother at home but now understood what her mother's job involved.

Sometimes, as in Melissa's case, the student succeeds in finding a topic. However, if Melissa had not found a topic of her own, Mrs. Loew would have had her choose a topic from her list and spend several days writing about that topic (see Graves on nudges, Chapter 6). Mrs. Loew wanted Melissa to know that she had something important to say, but she also made it clear that Melissa was expected to move forward with her writing.

A few struggling writers may not even be willing to start a topic list or to identify any possible topics for writing. In these cases, after all other options have been exhausted, the teacher will take the initiative of assigning the student a topic. The teacher makes it clear that the topic has been assigned because the student has not come up with a topic, despite the time and options allowed. After the topic is assigned, the teacher monitors the student's progress to see that the piece is drafted. If the student decides on a new topic, that can be pursued next. By taking these steps, the teacher makes it clear that the student can and will be a productive writer. Not writing is not an available option.

Putting Words on Paper

Paul, another student in Mrs. Loew's class, represented another type of struggling writer. Paul had many ideas for topics, which he could discuss at length. However, he had great difficulty putting his ideas down on paper. Paul knew initial consonant sounds, but his spelling was poor. He spent most of his time during the writers' workshop making detailed drawings.

Paul wanted to write about going fishing with his father. Mrs. Loew began the conference by showing Paul how to make a web of the information to be included in his story: how he and his father got up early in the morning, how they drove to the harbor to meet his father's friends, how they went far out to sea in the boat, the kinds of fish they caught, and so on. Mrs. Loew recorded the information on the web, then turned the page over to Paul. She helped him to phrase the beginning of the story, turning his oral language into the words he would put down in writing. They decided that the story would begin with the sentence, *One morning I got up very early to go fishing with my dad.* Mrs. Loew wrote this first sentence of the draft for Paul.

Then she helped him phrase his second sentence, *We put our poles and food in the car.* Mrs. Loew turned the paper and pencil over to Paul and helped him to start the sentence. She assured Paul that it was alright to use invented spelling in his draft, then left him alone for a few minutes. When Mrs. Loew returned, Paul had finished that sentence, and she helped him phrase and start writing the next sentence.

Mrs. Loew found that Paul would work well when she was close at hand and available to help, but he could not continue on his own for long. She taught three other students how to assist Paul by helping him to phrase the sentence he would be writing next and by cueing him to say each word slowly and put down the sounds he could hear. These students took turns working alongside Paul as he drafted his piece. Mrs. Loew stressed to Paul that he was responsible for getting his words down on paper, that other people would help but would not write for him. Paul progressed slowly, but by the second semester he was able to draft on his own.

A struggling writer like Paul puts a lot of time and effort into completing a first draft. Such a student is often reluctant to do any revising and editing. To give these students a sense of revising editing, without overwhelming them, teachers may take the following steps. First, students may be asked if there is a word or phrase they would like to add. Second, students can be shown how to circle a sentence and draw an arrow to show where it is to be moved. These two simple forms of revision do not require much effort and help to show students that revision need not be a painful process.

Editing may be daunting to these struggling writers because their drafts usually contain many words written in invented spelling. Teachers can make editing manageable for struggling writers by asking them to correct just a few of the words on their own. The words chosen for correction might be either words important in the students' piece (for example, the word *fishing* in Paul's piece) or common words likely to be useful to the student (for example, the word *with*). Or the teacher might ask the student which two or three words he or she would like to learn how to spell correctly. After the words have been identified, the student is instructed to circle all examples of these words and to write their correct spelling above. The teacher or a peer editor takes the responsibility for correcting other misspelled words. The teacher then instructs the student to add the newly learned words to his or her personal dictionary. In the future, the student is expected to refer to the dictionary in order to spell these words correctly.

As these examples suggest, struggling writers can be helped to progress in the writers' workshop with help from both the teacher and peers. Struggling writers benefit when they understand that they have something meaningful to say and that they can learn to put their ideas down on paper. Teachers give students ways of getting their writing started, then they work to build their confidence and independence as writers. ✳

References

Graves, D. (1983). *Writing: Teachers and children at work.* Exeter, NH: Heinemann.

Routman, R. (1991). *Invitations: Changing as teachers and learners K-12.* Portsmouth, NH: Heinemann.

not be asked to read short paragraphs and answer multiple-choice questions, because this is a contrived activity not typical in the real world. Wiggins argues that authentic assessments occur in rich contexts. He writes:

> A context is rich if it supports multiple approaches, styles, and solutions and requires good judgments in achieving an effective result. One must please a real audience, make a design actually work, or achieve an aesthetic effect that causes pride or dismay in the result. (p. 27)

The terms *authentic assessment* and *performance assessment* are sometimes used interchangeably, but the two represent different ideas. As Meyer (1992) points out, performance assessment has to do with the type of student response being assessed, while authentic assessment has to do with the context in which the response takes place. Authentic assessment always involves some sort of performance, but a performance assessment does not have to be authentic.

Here is an example of a performance assessment that is not also an authentic assessment. To assess reading comprehension, Teacher A designs a two-day procedure. On the first day, she assigns students a short story to read and gives them five questions to answer. The students spend a day reading and taking notes on the story, and a day writing answers to the questions. Students' reading ability is assessed on the basis of the answers they turn in.

In contrast, in an authentic assessment of reading, Teacher B conducts a conference with each student in her class to select the written responses from the students' literature response logs to be rated for the purposes of assessment. The responses represent writing in response to literature done all year in the daily readers' workshop.

Teacher A's procedure is an example of a performance assessment, because students must demonstrate that they can read by actually reading and writing about their understanding, rather than by answering multiple-choice questions. As Wiggins (1993) states, performance means executing a task and bringing it to completion. Students' ability to perform can only be assessed when they produce work, using their knowledge and skills in a particular context. Teacher A's case, however, is not an example of authentic assessment, because the context is contrived.

Teacher B's case is also an example of a performance assessment, because it looks at reading in terms of students' performance, in this case, samples taken from their literature response logs. Teacher B's procedure shows authentic assessment, because performance reflects the ongoing conditions for learning in the classroom. Assessment in Teacher A's classroom is much more test-like than in Teacher B's classroom. As Wiggins (1989) points out, truly authentic assessments often do not involve contrived tests.

Performance assessment may involve students in creating their own tasks, not just in carrying out tasks dictated by others. These assessments may require students to analyze their own performance and to reflect upon their own learning. In contrast to traditional forms of assessment, students are likely to have much more involvement in and control over the assessment process.

Authentic assessment is meaningful to students. Students find the assessment engaging, although the task need not be of immediate practical value. For example, depending upon the context, an authentic assessment may involve the writing of poetry. Authentic assessment is not limited to obviously utilitarian tasks, such as having students write letters to request information. ✳

References

Meyer, C. A. (1992). What's the difference between authentic and performance assessment? *Educational Leadership, 49* (8), 39-40.

Wiggins, G. (1989). Teaching to the (authentic) test. *Educational Leadership, 46* (7), 41-47.

Wiggins, G. (1992). Creating tests worth taking. *Educational Leadership, 49* (8), 26-33.

Wiggins, G. (1993). Assessment: Authenticity, context, and validity. *Phi Delta Kappan, 75* (3), 200-214.

learning over the course of the year, teachers will want to use documentation portfolios (see previous article for a description of each type of portfolio). In this case, because portfolios will not be scored, the contents may vary from one student's portfolio to the next, reflecting differences in the work accomplished by different students. If the purpose is to gather information on the effectiveness of new forms of instruction, however, evaluation portfolios are more appropriate. The items in these portfolios will need to be standardized, so that a common scoring system can be applied.

Teachers may be in schools or districts where benchmarks are being used (see Reading Benchmarks in this chapter and Writing Benchmarks in Chapter 12). If so, specific pieces of student work can be used to show evidence for the benchmarks. For example, if one goal or benchmark is to interpret the author's message, students and teachers can be alert to evidence that the student knows how to do this. The student could be asked to look through her literature response journal for entries that included an interpretation of the author's message in a story. The teacher could look through her anecdotal records for instances when the student discussed the author's message and did a good job of thinking it through. These pieces of evidence would then be considered for the student's portfolio, and those selected would be placed in the portfolio and marked in some way (such as with a post-it) to identify why they were included.

The work collected in a portfolio may take many different forms—it may be written (e.g., written responses to literature, lists of books read, research reports, writing samples), created in an art medium (e.g., drawings or paintings done in response to literature, illustrations in student-published books, posters or other artwork for research reports, student-designed book jackets), audio- or videotaped (e.g., tapes of discussions, presentations, dramatic performances, or reading aloud), or photographed (e.g., photos of large projects or three-dimensional pieces), or it may be the videotape, audiotape, or photograph itself created by the student as part of his or her work. Besides student work products, a student's self-evaluations and goals, reflections, and teacher records (e.g., anecdotal records, status of the class, running records) may be included in the portfolio.

Students' reflections can give teachers (and the students themselves) insights into the processes of learning. One way to include this is to schedule a weekly class discussion during which students reflect on their learning experiences. For example, students can be given 10 to 15 minutes every Friday to reflect on the week's work and choose something they would like to share with their classmates about their learning. The teacher might want to prompt students by asking one or two of the following questions the first few times the group meets for reflection:

- What went well for you this week? What didn't go well? Why?

- What new and interesting things did you learn?

- What did you learn about yourself? For example, did you discover strengths, new skills, growing interests, definite dislikes? How can this information be useful to you?

- Did anything help you learn better? If so, what was it, and why do you think it helped?

- Did anything make it harder for you to learn? If so, do you have ideas for making learning easier for yourself in the future?

Reflections on specific pieces of work also are valuable. Students can fill in an entry slip (see Figure 11.2 for an example) for each item they put in their portfolios. Another possibility is to have students fill in a reflection sheet occasionally for an item that took a lot of work, such as a major project. Questions on the reflection sheet might ask:

1. Why did you choose this item? What was important about it to you?

2. What do you feel you learned by doing this piece of work (about the topic *and* about yourself)?

3. Did you try something new in this piece of work? How did it it come out?

Figuro 11.2 ENTRY SLIP FOR PORTFOLIO ITEMS

Entry Slip
Name _____   Date _____
Description of item _____
I chose this item for my portfolio because _____
_____
_____
_____

marks below reflect the practices suggested in this text for readers' workshop, defining what a typical elementary student would be expected to do by the end of the school year (see also Figure 11.3 for a classroom checklist).

Benchmarks for the Readers' Workshop

- Enjoys reading
- Chooses to read for own purposes
- Shares books with others `
- Participates in reading discussions

Figure 11.3   CLASSROOM CHECKLIST WITH READING BENCHMARKS

- Understands story vocabulary

- Applies multiple cue systems to decode unfamiliar words

- Writes in response to reading:
  - aesthetic responses (explains feelings/reactions, interprets theme/author's message, makes personal connections to reading)

  - efferent responses (knows characters, setting, problem, events, and resolution in stories; knows main idea and supporting details in expository text)

- Understands different genres and their characteristics

- Understands elements of author's craft

- Sets goals and evaluates own achievement of reading

- Instructional reading level average for grade

From a set of benchmarks such as this, teachers need to decide how a particular benchmark can be interpreted for their grade level. For example, a kindergarten teacher might expect students to respond aesthetically by drawing or writing about their favorite parts of a story. A second-grade teacher might expect students to describe what they thought the author's message was in a story, while a fourth-grade teacher might expect students not only to tell about the author's message but to make a connection between that message and their own lives.

Teachers also need to determine how much evidence constitutes achievement of the benchmark. For the above items, for example, the teachers might decide there should be two good examples each semester in the child's portfolio. Teachers of younger students will have to take on more of the responsibility for finding good examples of evidence for the portfolios, while teachers of older students can give much of that responsibility to the students themselves.

A fifth-grade teacher decided to do this by meeting with a small group of students to show them what she considered good examples of evidence for several different benchmarks. These "anchor pieces" were exemplary student examples selected from the previous year's class, so that students could see the quality of work the teacher expected. She used a chart similar to the one in Figure 11.4 to show them where to look for evidence. The students then gathered examples from their own work to share and discuss with the group. They were given post-its to "tag" their examples with the benchmark represented. This tagging process helped keep the portfolios more orderly. Each member of this group then met with a small group of other students to explain the process and help their classmates make appropriate choices for

volunteers can be trained to take careful observational notes and fill in checklists. A teacher may want to make arrangements with a fellow teacher to come in and observe the class when she is instructing. Some teachers may find this intimidating at first, but observations that focus on what students are doing in response to the teacher's instruction can be extremely helpful for a teacher who wants feedback. ✳

References

Goodman, Y. M. (1985). Kidwatching: Observing children in the classroom. In A. Jaggar & M. T. Smith-Burke (Eds.), *Observing the language learner* (pp. 9-18). Newark DE: International Reading Association.

Connections to the Home and Community

Connections to the home and community in the area of assessment look different when teachers follow a balanced literacy approach. In traditional school systems, parents receive a report card with subject grades for older students and skills and work habits grades for younger students, while the community sees a school's standardized test scores published in the local newspaper. Teachers of readers' and writers' workshops need to give parents and the community additional information on which to evaluate the effectiveness of these programs and students' achievements.

Background

Parents who expect teachers to follow the patterns of instruction the parents themselves experienced when they attended school can feel confused by newer approaches such as literature-based instruction and the process approach to writing. Norma Mickelson (1992) believes that good communication bridges that gap when parents are told the philosophy underlying the program, how those beliefs lead to classroom practices, and how student learning is evaluated. She suggests that teachers ask parents to become partners in the evaluation of their child's progress. This can be accomplished through:

- asking parents what goals they have for their child;

- asking parents to observe their child in order to help teachers understand the home and community environment;

- inviting parents to conferences to discuss mutual goals for their child, progress toward those goals, and future plans; and

- working with parents to find a mutually acceptable reporting procedure that gives parents the kind of information they feel they need as well as an understanding of the kind of information the teacher wants to share.

Procedure

Teachers should inform parents early in the school year about the assessment system the class will be using. The class newsletter is a good vehicle for this (see a sample in Connections to the Home and Community, Chapter 9). In the newsletter, the teacher can explain what portfolios are and why he has chosen to use them in the classroom. He can include a list of benchmarks and a brief explanation of why they were chosen. He can describe how anecdotal records are taken, give some examples, and ask interested parents to note literacy behaviors they see at home and share their observations with him.

As students gain more knowledge about the assessment system and how it works for them, they can write articles for later issues of the newsletter. A student's thoughts about how she is putting together her portfolio to showcase her work and demonstrate her abilities can do much to convey the purpose of the system as well as the actual practices. Samples of student work and data collection forms can help make the message clearer and more concrete. The teacher should ask students if any would like to volunteer to have some of their book logs, responses to literature, etc. included. This communication with parents should be ongoing, just as the assessment system is.

Open house is another excellent opportunity to share the assessment system with parents. During an open house, the teacher and students might collaborate on a presentation of the readers' and writers' workshops. The teacher could start out by explaining the philosophy behind the program and how students will be evaluated. Groups of students follow up by describing and possibly demonstrating particular components. For example, different groups could handle book talks, literature discussion groups, written and visual responses to literature, peer writing conferences, revising and editing, and so forth. Afterward, each student escorts his or her parents around the room to view learning centers, the class library, or other areas up close and to answer questions. Students also take time to show their families their own work and accomplishments.

Individual conferences allow parents to find out about a child's development in depth. One conference technique used successfully is the *student-led parent conference* (Austin, 1994). As the name implies, students take the role of conference leader. Terri Austin and her sixth-grade students developed this type of conference after Austin realized her former system of assessment no longer matched her holistic instruction. She taught her students how to prepare to lead a conference as a natural outgrowth of their increased responsibility for learning in her classroom. She described four steps students needed to complete in preparation (Austin, 1994, p. 29):

1. Identifying common values, particularly the concrete characteristics of a "good student."

2. Assembling the components of the conference portfolio by gathering information about themselves as learners.

3. Participating in a teacher-student conference to discuss the results of the data gathered and to complete the report card.

4. Conducting a practice conference and receiving feedback.

In the weeks before the conference, students reviewed their work, chose their best pieces, wrote reflections, evaluated their efforts, and organized their portfolios to show what and how they were learning. Through these experiences, the students wrestled with the same issues their teacher did when faced with assessing learning—how to show not only the result of learning, but the process the learner experienced and growth in less tangible skills (e.g., reasoning, analyzing, etc.).

Prior to the conference, parents were asked to fill in a parent comment sheet that asked what parents thought about their child as a reader, writer, scientist, and mathematician at home. Other teachers who worked with the students, such as the reading specialist or the librarian, could fill out a similar form. Students used the information in their conferences and the forms were included in their portfolios.

During conference time, the students presented their work for the quarter to their parents. They asked their parents to read selected pieces of work and explained how and why they were created. Since students were given time to practice and receive feedback from the teacher and peers, their presentations were not more difficult than they could manage. The students themselves reported feeling more at ease the second time they conduct their conferences. The teacher's role was minimal during the actual conference, largely because of the preparation she did earlier with her students.

Having students share their portfolios with other classes is a good way for the students to practice conducting a conference. Ideally, the students from the other class also keep portfolios. Each student finds a partner from the other class (or the teachers can assign partners), and the two sit together to hear about each other's work. Austin's sixth-grade students listened to a third-grade class practice their conferences. Later, they met with another sixth grade to practice theirs. Sharing their accomplishments with the school community outside of their classroom helps students see their learning as part of a larger literacy effort. ✳

References

Austin, T. (1994). *Changing the view: Student-led parent conferences.* Portsmouth, NH: Heinemann.

Mickelson, N. I. (1992). Evaluation in whole language: Interacting with parents. In K. S. Goodman, L. B. Bird, & Y. M. Goodman (Eds.), *The whole language catalog supplement on authentic assessment* (p. 129). Macmillan/McGraw-Hill.

Troubleshooting: What About Standardized Tests?

Assessment provides information to different groups, or stakeholders, concerned with children's reading progress (Farr, 1992). The portfolio assessment we described in this chapter is important to teachers as it informs their daily decisions about instruction. It is important to students because they must understand their own strengths and needs if their literacy skills are to improve. Parents are interested in portfolio assessment because they want to monitor their children's progress and take an active part in their education. Administrators look to these measures to compare students' performance with the school's curriculum.

Another group, members of the general public, usually require broader means of assessing student achievement. These are the people who judge school's effectiveness and determine if education dollars are wisely spent. This group usually turns to *norm-reference*, standardized tests for information. Administrators, parents, and teachers use the results of standardized tests to compare their children's performance with others across the nation.

Criticism of Standardized Tests

Typically, standardized tests are administered to large groups of students, have a multiple-choice format with only one correct answer, and are machine scored. The raw scores from these tests are interpreted into percentile ranks, stanines, and grade equivalents. Reading tests usually contain subtests of decoding, comprehension, and vocabulary. In recent years, standardized tests have come under a high degree of criticism from educators. Robert Tierney and colleagues (1991) discuss four problems with these kinds of tests:

(1) *They reflect an outdated view of classrooms and restricted goals for learning.*
Reading programs of the past contained text passages with artificial controls on vocabulary. Accompanying workbooks required marking correct answers or responding with a few words. Today's programs are literature based and students work together to discuss books and construct meanings. Extended written responses have replaced workbooks. Standardized tests are not consistent with current practices.

(2) *They reflect a limited view of reading and writing.*
Most test publishers have not responded to the current perspective that reading is a meaning-constructing process in which skills are integrated, not isolated. They overlook the complexities of reading abilities reducing them to a total score.

(3) *They disenfranchise teachers and constrain instructional possibilities.*
When too much importance is given to standardized tests, teachers may loose faith in their abilities to make instructional decisions based on the needs of their students. Teacher's instructional time may be guided by someone else's test, limiting students' learning and decision-making opportunities.

(4) *They do not engage students in self-assessment.*
Instead of empowering learning and teaching the tests are detached from it. Students' views of progress are not considered.

Problems with our current standardized tests are obvious, yet we can be encouraged by cooperative efforts currently underway that should lead to an improvement of future reading assessment measures. But right now, many teachers must deal with an annually administered test that reflects the problems noted above. An important segment of the community may use the results to judge their students and their reading. This is a group that often makes decisions that affect classroom curriculum and materials.

A Sensible Approach

Jeanne Reardon (1990) offers a pragmatic approach when she suggests that teachers "put reading tests in their place." She notes that she has never found standardized tests results useful, nor have her students. Still, it is difficult to dismiss them because scores often determine the school system's support for her classroom program and the kinds of reading materials she may select. So, to assure that students do as well as possible, she takes about a week just prior to the testing to present reading tests as a genre. She focuses only on the comprehension component of the tests, not on subtests such as phonics or vocabulary, because she acknowledges the importance of reading comprehension.

Reardon's students are active participants in their classroom literacy community. Much of each day is spent reading and discussing quality literature. They understand the characteristics of many literary genres so, Reardon believes, it is possible to teach the reading-test genre in an intellectually honest way that does not violate her beliefs about language learning. She does not make it seem special, but rather presents it in much the same way as any other genre. She named the genre *reading-test reading* in order that it could be talked about and distinguished from other forms of written language.

To introduce the form, Reardon gives each student a paper with two sample passages. She asks the children to read the passages and write about what they noticed. Then they discuss their findings. After the discussion, Reardon

Figure 11.6   READING-TEST READING

Reading-Test Reading

- You can tell it's a reading test by the way it looks.

- There aren't any pictures.

- It tells you what to do.

- It asks questions. You have to choose from the answers, and you can only choose one answer.

- All the writing on the page doesn't go together.

- It's just short pieces of writing, not the whole thing, so it doesn't have to make sense. (It's hard to understand.)

- You're not supposed to think about what it means to you, just answer the question.

- It's tricky. It's like a puzzle or a code.

- It doesn't have any author.

summarizes their findings in a list like the one shown in Figure 11.6.

Over the next few days, as one activity within their readers' workshop, the students work through a few more practice passages on their own. They discuss and debate items in this puzzle-like genre with friends, just as they are used to talking about good literature. In order to keep the power with the children, Reardon does not ask them to read the practice tests in silence and isolation. That would give the test the power to judge the correct responses rather than giving children the power to discover meaning for themselves.

Reardon explains that once children understand the genre, they control it. The children recognize it as a trivial form of writing that has no special significance in their lives. Their confidence as readers and meaning makers remains. The power of the test is diminished.

When standardized tests have important implications for teachers and students, an approach like Reardon's is a sensible one. Teachers cannot let standardized tests dictate their curriculum, nor can they disregard them. Until we have reading assessment measures that are acceptable to all stake-holders, teachers must explore solutions that do not compromise their beliefs or limit the learning opportunities available to their students. ✳

References

Farr, R. (1992). Putting it all together: Solving the reading assessment puzzle. *The Reading Teacher, 46*, 26-37.

Reardon, S. J. (1990). Putting reading tests in their place. *The New Advocate, 3*, 29-37.

Tierney, R. J., Carter, M. A., & Desai, L. E. (1991). *Portfolio assessment in the reading-writing classroom*. Norwood, MA: Christopher-Gordon Publishers, Inc

Chapter 12

EVALUATING PROGRESS IN THE WRITERS' WORKSHOP

The Impact of Jane Hansen: Literacy Portfolios

The approach to literacy portfolios developed by Jane Hansen (1992) and her colleagues has the aim of helping students to know themselves better and to feel valued as people. Teachers, as well as students of all ages, can put together literacy portfolios.

Scott, a fourth grader, included the items listed below in his literacy portfolio. Scott commented about each of these items to one of his teachers.

- A drawing. "This shows that I can draw pictures, because before I couldn't draw. I'll always remember this. At home my mother used to give me paper and pencil, and I broke the pencils and crossed my arms. Now I write."

- A draft of a piece of writing he had published as a book in the resource room the previous year. "This is the first book I wrote. I can write books."

- A piece of writing from the current year. "Before I couldn't write that good, and now I can. Now I can write better and read better."

- A list of books he can read. "This says that I'm a reader, that I can read these books."

- A book, *The Litte Engine That Could.* "This is one of my favorite books. My mom used to read it to me." (Hansen, 1992, p. 66)

Setting Up a Portfolio System

Teachers who choose portfolios as a means to reflect students' growth in literacy, will want to develop a plan for implementing this form of assessment. They must consider what will be placed in the portfolios, who the portfolios will serve, and how the portfolios will be used. They must plan instruction that ensures portfolios become an integral part of their classroom literacy program.

Background

Jane Hansen (1992a) describes how a teacher's ongoing instruction creates a firm foundation for the successful use of literacy portfolios (for another view of setting up a portfolio system see Chapter 11). She identifies five skills that students need if they are to use portfolios effectively. Teachers will want to provide the instruction and opportunities necessary to help students develop these skills:

- To consider possibilities and make choices.

- To make selections about what is important.

- To recognize that something is unclear and that assistance or further study is necessary.

- To work independently and with peers without adult supervision.

- To examine work products and find value in them.

Procedure

The writers' workshop supports students' development of the skills Hansen suggests are needed to make literacy portfolios an important assessment tool. It is helpful for teachers to recognize how portfolios can be a natural extension of the workshop experience. Within the writers' workshop students regularly consider and choose topics for their writing pieces. They decide how to develop their ideas and make plans for what to do next. They learn of the choices, and reasons for choices, made by their teacher and classmates. Literacy portfolios require students to make choices.

During the workshop, teachers share their own writing and the literature of others focusing on the importance of the piece to the writer and the reader. Students consider significant events in their own lives on which to focus their writing. When students confer and share their work they want to know if their writing reflects their intent. What seems important? What is memorable for the reader? Literacy portfolios require that students consider what is important.

As teachers and students confer together, in small, and in large groups they work collaboratively to solve a variety of writing concerns. The teacher's attention to problem solving emphasizes its value and encourages students to request help when they are stuck. The teacher's approach also provides a positive model for peer conferences. Students will learn to listen carefully to one another's writing to answer for example, "Can you tell that Jake is really scared?" or to ask, "Why didn't your mom want you to go to your friend's house? I didn't understand that part." Literacy portfolios require that students be reflective. They should recognize when they need help and understand that there is always more they can learn.

Student ownership is central to the writers' workshop. As teachers work with individuals and small groups, they trust that students will be productively engaged, make appropriate choices, and that they take their work and that of their classmates seriously. Literacy portfolios require that students believe their judgments are trusted.

When teachers establish a literacy portfolio system, they show students the value of carefully examining one's own writing. Teachers do this by sharing their own portfolios with their students. They comment on the portfolio itself. It may be a folder of the type students will use, or it may be a personal container because students, too, will create or choose their own forms of portfolios. Teachers discuss the contents of their portfolios, perhaps a letter from a family member, a list of favorite books, a piece written with the class, and reminder notes. They share the explanations they have written telling why each piece was chosen and what the piece reveals about them as writers. Then they share what they plan to try next, their goals for the future. They solicit students' comments and questions about their portfolios.

After the mini-lesson to introduce the notion of portfolios, students are invited to think about themselves as writers. What important items would they include in a portfolio? What would those items show about them? On this first day teachers may ask students to begin reflecting by looking through their writing folders to list possible items with, perhaps, brief notes about their importance. To provide more guidance, some teachers brainstorm a general list with students and ask that they choose from the list. Other teachers specify certain requirements such as: include at least two different forms of writing; include one piece that you have written outside of school. Young children often choose best pieces of writing based on content for example, "I had fun at my cousin's birthday," rather than pieces that reflect growth. Their teachers may want to specify that of three selections the child and teacher must agree on one.

Teachers will need to consider the form students' reflections might take. As young children talk about their selections, teachers can record anecdotal notes. By year's end, these children may be prepared to write their own reflections. Some teachers ask students to reflect on each selection; others ask students to write a letter to them in which they discuss the overall contents of their portfolios. (Students take their letters through the writing process to enhance the thought and content of their reflections.) Their ideas may be guided by the questions: What do you do well as a writer? What's the most recent thing you've learned to do as a writer? What do you want to learn next in order to be a better writer? How do you intend to go about learning how to do that? (Hansen, 1992b).

Students are given regular time during writers' workshop to make selections, write reflections and goals, and share their portfolio choices with classmates. As the school year progresses and the writing community develops, teachers and students may continually revise their portfolios. As goals are met, new things are added, and items are removed. Some teachers prefer to set a schedule for portfolio work. Time may be allotted each month or every six weeks to "visit" the portfolios. Often the schedule is organized around the school's reporting periods.

Teachers find that portfolios provide them with a rich understanding of students' development. Each product reveals something unique about the writer and each collection of pieces speaks of learning over time. Student's reflections reveal their thought processes and how they view themselves as writers. Teachers gain information as they observe students' choices and talk with students individually and in groups during the selection and reflection processes. Many teachers also schedule times during the year to meet individually with students about their portfolios. Before reporting periods they may ask that students "complete" their portfolios and prepare to present them. As a part of the completion process students make sure the content of their portfolios is up to date and they confer with peers about their letters and presentations. Teachers usually request that the portfolios be turned in before individual conferences. Then teachers have an opportunity to review them and make notes, often using a record-keeping form. During the conferences students present their work; teachers record their observations, and ask clarifying questions. Then, together, they consider both the students' individual goals and the goals the teacher may recommend. This portfolio review usually occurs before reporting periods so it is convenient for parents to be involved in the process. Students may share their portfolios at home or the students may share them during parent conferences (see Connections to the Home and Community, Chapter 11).

Self-evaluation is an important part of the writers' workshop. Literacy portfolios provide a tool to help students become thoughtful evaluators from year to year as they carry their portfolios from grade to grade—and beyond. Our hope is that the evaluation process will extend throughout their lifetimes because, of course, we expect that they will always continue to learn and grow as writers. ✳

References

Hansen, J. (1992a). Literacy portfolios emerge. *The Reading Teacher, 45,* 604-607.

Hansen, J. (1992b). Teachers evaluate their own literacy. In D. H. Graves & B. S. Sunstein (Eds.), *Portfolio portraits* (pp. 73-81). Portsmouth, NH: Heinemann.

Resource

Hansen, J., & Staley, K. (1994). Video. *Portfolios: Students as readers, writers, and evaluators.* Portsmouth, NH: Heinemann.

Writing Benchmarks

Benchmarks are a means to monitor and report on student learning. *Grade level benchmarks* are statements that reflect expectations for the hypothetical average student at the end of the grade level. When teachers use benchmarks to interpret and evaluate portfolio information, they gain a fuller understanding of each student's literacy development.

Background

Throughout history, educators have used terms such as behavioral objectives and standards to describe literacy expectations for students. Behavioral objectives are usually written quite specifically—for example, begins sentences with capital letters. In 1996, the International Reading Association and the National Council of Teachers of English published a list of twelve standards aimed at fostering higher levels of literacy for students in grades K-12 (NCTE, 1996). These standards are presented in broad statements. For example, the standard specifically centered on writing says, "Students employ a wide range of strategies as they write and use different writing process elements appropriately to communicate with different audiences for a variety of purposes." Whereas, while teachers often find the specificity of objectives to be overly prescriptive not permitting responsiveness to the needs of their particular students, broadly written standards may seem unclear and difficult to assess.

Kathryn Au et al. (1990) suggests the use of benchmarks to define expectations for student learning. Benchmarks are presented in language more specific than that of the English Language Arts Standards, but they are not as detailed as the usual behavioral objectives. Au also believes the term benchmark to be more flexible than the term standard. Benchmarks do not convey a sense of "truth for all time" but rather the notion that things do change.

Au led a group of teachers and other educators who shared common understandings of children, curriculum, and classroom practices in developing a set of benchmarks to evaluate the literacy achievement of students with whom they worked. To be sure their goals were in line with those of the nation and their community they also reviewed (1) the school district's curriculum guides, (2) the standardized achievement test administered by their schools, and (3) the scope and sequence charts of several recently published basal reading programs. They set their expectations high and agreed to evaluate each student to determine if they were performing at, above, or below grade level. They expected students, by year's end, to perform across a range of grade levels.

Students were introduced to the benchmarks during the goal-setting process. Teachers explained that the benchmarks were their own for students' learning and that the instruction they provided would help them meet those goals. As students worked on their portfolios they sometimes set goals for themselves that were similar to the benchmarks; other times they chose different or more specific goals.

Procedure

Teachers wanting to develop a set of literacy benchmarks will need to consider their curriculum along with expectations for student achievement. To begin this process they will want to reference the expectations of their state and school district, their curriculum guides, and standardized- and criterion-referenced assessment measures used in their school. They will

Figure 12.1 WRITING BENCHMARKS CHECKLIST

Writing Benchmarks	Enjoys writing	Chooses to write for own purposes	Shares writing with others	Selects own topics and plans for writing	Writes from own experiences	Writes in a variety of forms (e.g., personal narratives, fiction, poetry, letters, research reports)	Uses interesting language in own writing	Confers and revises	Edits (for spelling, mechanics, grammar, paragraphs) and publishes	Uses elements of author's craft	Sets goals and evaluates own achievement of writing	Holistic quality of writing (meets grade level expectations)

laboration with students' review of their portfolios. In addition to the portfolios, students' writing folders (see Figure 7.7) provide evidence as to whether the benchmarks have been met.

Teachers who use benchmarks to evaluate students' progress usually find the system offers them new insights and growth as professionals. As they examine results they may note general areas of weakness for most students, groups of students, or for individual students. These patterns of needs can guide instructional planning directed at addressing the needs of these students. On the other hand, teachers may find that they have aimed a benchmark too low. If most students achieve a particular goal before year's end, the teacher may want to heighten his expectations for that benchmark. As teachers work with benchmarks, they also develop a fuller understanding of them. For example, their overall sense of an "at-grade-level" piece of writing is formed as they continually reflect upon students' works. Teachers often choose anchor pieces and use them to determine holistic quality of writing, or average writing for a grade level. It is expected that these anchor pieces will be challenged and changed as teachers grow in their understanding of students' capabilities and as their own instructional practices evolve. ❋

References

Au, K. H., Scheu, J. A., Kawakami, A., & Herman, P. A. (1990). Assessment and accountability in a whole literacy curriculum. *The Reading Teacher, 43,* 574-578.

NCTE & IRA (1996). *Standards for the English language arts.* Urbana, IL: National Council of Teachers of English.

Valencia, S. W., Hiebert, E. H., and Afflerbach, P. P. (Eds.). (1994). *Authentic reading assessment: Practices and possibilities.* Newark, DE: International Reading Association.

Status of the Class

A *status of the class* gives teachers a record of what students are doing and have done during writers' workshop. The *status sheet* is usually a teacher-prepared grid with a list of students' names down the left side and boxes for each day of the week by each name. Teachers use the information they record to plan instruction and to track student growth and development. As children listen to their classmate's plans, they learn of options they may want to try out in their own writing.

Background

One of the first teachers to write about the status of the class was Nancie Atwell (1987). She found the procedure brought order to her middle school writers' workshops. The procedure has been adopted and adapted by many elementary teachers.

Atwell suggested introducing the status of the class during a mini-lesson on the second day of writers' workshop. During the lesson she explained to students the purpose of the procedure and introduced the types of responses they might make when called upon. She presented appropriate terminology so they could answer quickly and concisely. Following each day's status report, Atwell had a verbal contract with every student. Students said what they would do and she had their plans recorded. Keeping the weekly charts over time, Atwell noted patterns for individuals and for groups of students that helped to guide the instructional support she provided.

Procedure

Teachers usually find it best to take a class status right after the mini-lesson while children are still together in a large group. When students become familiar with the procedure it should take no more than three minutes.

To introduce status of the class a teacher might say, "Every day before we begin writing I'll ask each of you to tell me your writing plans for the day so I'll know how best to help you. Some of you will want to continue drafting the piece you began yesterday. Maybe you will want to read your piece and make changes or revisions. Perhaps you need to talk or confer with someone to get new ideas for your piece, or maybe the topic you chose yesterday wasn't a good one for you and you'd like to begin a new piece. Be sure to listen carefully as others share. You'll learn what they are doing and maybe you'll get some new ideas for your own writing." As students' pieces develop over time the teacher will introduce other ways to respond such as, "I need help with editing today," or "I will publish 'Lost at the Zoo.'"

When teachers review their status sheets they often find the need to provide special assistance, perhaps to a student like Cindi who begins writing a new piece every day. Or they may discover that several students could benefit from a group conference on something like adding details to stories.

They may also find evidence that students are learning from one another. Patti's report that she was editing for "talking marks" may have encouraged Mindy's and Lisa's interest in adding dialogue. Teachers can heighten interest in other's ideas during status reports by occasionally introducing new questions such as "How did you get the idea for your story?" or "Why is it helpful for you to confer with [student's name]?" ✳

Reference

Atwell, N. (1987). *In the middle: Writing, reading, and learning with adolescents.* Portsmouth, NH: Heinemann.

Figure 12.3   A TEACHER'S STATUS OF THE CLASS SHEET

CLASS STATUS SHEET: WRITING WORKSHOP

NP=New Piece D=Drafting R=Revising C=Conferencing E=Editing P=Publishing

Week of 2/5

Students	M	T	W	TH	F
Sam	NP "Fishing"	D.	D	D/Cw/Matt	R
Arletta	P Computer	P Illustration	Share pub. NP	D - Birthday Party	D
Ramón	ab.	C w/ Tony D Irish attic	R	R	E
Mindy	EC w/ Patti	C w/me ~ marks	EC w/Patti	Final E Con P	D
Leslie	P	P Share P	NP (cont) C w/Dari	D Andy	D
Cindi	NP ?	NP - sister	ab	N.P. dog	C w/me
Edward	E	EC w/Jamie E	Final E Begin P	P	P
Matt	R Museum visit	R	E	C w/Sam	E
Eric	D Baseball	D	R	NP abandoned	ab.
Patti	EC w/Mindy D - Body	R adding dialogue	EC w/Mindy D	D	E
Jackson	ab.	Final E Con P.	P	D Missing Share P	D
Nicole	Finish P read to kids	NP. Piece ideas	D	C w/me D	D
Mistry	NP - poem	D poem	D	R	R
Lurita	D Baby Go!	D	D	Try story as a poem	D. poem
Steven	P Dinner at Home	ab.	P	P Share ?	NP - ? Jose
Tony	Final E Con D	P	P Share P	NP. poem Words C	P. poem Words C
Jamie	D Grant 3	EC w/Ed D	D	C w/Nicole D	D
Lisa	D Voltaire giving	D	D	C w/Mindy to add ditto	R
Dari	D football soccer	D	C w/Leslie R - football game	R	E
Karl	P - will share today	NP ?	D Snow fight	D	D C(?)

Figure 12.4   STATUS OF THE CLASS FORM

CLASS STATUS SHEET: WRITING WORKSHOP

NP=New Place   D=Drafting   C=Conferencing   E=Editing   P=Publishing

Week of _____

Students	M	T	W	TH	F

Anecdotal Records

Anecdotal records are brief, informal observational notes that teachers make as they observe individual students. During the writers' workshop these notes may focus on the process in which students engage as well as their writing products. These dated notes, accumulated over time, help teachers make sense of what their students do as writers and provide a basis for discussing progress and setting instructional goals.

Background

Lynn Rhodes and Sally Nathenson-Mejia (1992) note that once teachers have developed a solid understanding of students' reading and writing, they appreciate the open-ended format of anecdotal records which furnish a means for capturing the richness of their students' literacy processes and products. They suggest that anecdotal records are specific, report rather than evaluate or interpret, and relate to other facts known about the child.

Teachers should analyze anecdotal records to make inferences about students' writing, look for developmental trends within individuals and across children, and identify strengths and weaknesses in both learning and teaching. Their analyses can guide instructional planning, inform students and parents about progress, and suggest new assessment questions for study.

Procedure

As teachers begin observing and taking anecdotal notes, they are often concerned about what to write. It is important to be selective and to record information not available elsewhere. It would be redundant to note information already saved in a draft or on a status of the class sheet. Some teachers find it helpful to narrow down their observations by making a reference list of items on which they want to focus. Specific items may pertain to writing behaviors, interests, purposes for writing, ownership, hypotheses made, engagement, interactions, and misconceptions.

Often teachers find it difficult to make time for observations within the context of their busy classrooms. A recording schedule may be helpful. Teachers can examine their plans to find times when students are working independently on literacy activities, and then select a certain number of children to observe each day. As the observation process becomes more routine, they will find it easier to record noteworthy events as they occur.

Teachers use a variety of means for recording observations. Some use clipboards with a class list; others use notebooks or file boxes. Sticky notes and peel-off labels work well as they can be carried easily and later placed on students' individual record forms (see Figure 12.5). Some teachers have found it convenient to use the same form to record the status of the class and their observational notes. The combined information presents an extended

Figure 12.5   A LABEL GRID FOR ANECDOTAL RECORDS

Name _____

Notes:

Reading	Writing

Form for use with computer mailing labels.

and discussed to show students what an excellent versus an average or below average piece of work looks or sounds like.

Grades should be used sparingly. Some teachers feel compelled to grade every piece of work a student does, fearing perhaps that students will not be motivated to complete assignments otherwise. Even if this is true, grades as motivation will not inspire students to become lifelong learners. In classrooms where readers' and writers' workshops are at the heart of literacy learning, students can find personal motivations that are more compelling. Since learning is a social act (see The Impact of Lev Vygotsky, Chapter 1), social motivators such as sharing ideas about a book you have read or reading your writing to someone else for feedback can be more meaningful than earning a grade for a reading or writing activity.

Teachers and students can work together to determine how many and which writing pieces or reading activities will be graded. With this knowledge, students may spend extra time on those examples. This means that teachers will grade the best products students can produce, which is a better evaluation of a student's performance than a composite grade based on every piece of work produced. For example, if students know only certain writing samples will be graded and they have some say in which ones are chosen, they may be willing to take more risks in their writing. These risky efforts may or may not work out, but students will certainly learn more from them than they would producing another safe, predictable piece. And regardless of whether students receive a grade for a piece of work, they should receive some form of response to it.

In addition, grades should not be the only means of communicating student performance. Portfolios are an excellent means for teachers and students to communicate a student's growth and accomplishments to parents (see Setting Up a Portfolio System in Chapters 11 and 12; Connections to the Home and Community in Chapter 11).

Many teachers choose to write a narrative to accompany the report card. (At some schools, this is the report card.) The narrative can be a valuable part of the assessment system when it communicates to parents and students how the teacher perceives the child as a learner. Information from both writers' and readers' workshop experiences can be combined to provide a clearer view of the student's growth in literacy. The teacher's anecdotal records and status of the class sheets; the students' work products, reflections, goals, and self-evaluations; and the parents' comment sheets are all potential sources for the narrative.

Another addition to (or replacement for) the traditional report card is a checklist. Teacher Caryl Crowell (1992) devised a checklist for her bilingual classroom from a list of learning behaviors she observed in students, the results of miscue analysis, and children's writing samples. The list (Crowell, 1992, p. 113), which serves as her benchmark, includes items for:

- oral language development (e.g., listens attentively to stories read aloud, explains thinking, talks about language),

- literature response (e.g., relates reading to personal experiences, retells and summarizes stories),

- writing (e.g., self-selects topics and ideas, writes for a variety of purposes and audiences, revises for clarity and meaning),

- writing mechanics (e.g., uses end punctuation appropriately, uses age-appropriate handwriting),

- spelling (e.g., invented spelling shows awareness of spelling patterns),

- learning in a social environment (e.g., uses room resources for information and clarification, is organized and has necessary materials),

- math problem solving (e.g., discusses problem-solving strategies), and

- second language development (e.g., listens attentively when second language is used).

Crowell rates each item on a scale of 1 to 4, with 1 representing *rarely* and 4, *often*. (She found that the typical categories of *always* and *never* did not apply to her classroom.) The checklist, which accompanies the quarterly report card, has space for parent comments. She revises her checklist each year as her knowledge about children's learning and literacy acquisition grows. ✳

References

Crowell, C. G. (1992). A whole language checklist. In K. S. Goodman, L. B. Bird, & Y. M. Goodman (Eds.), *The whole language catalog supplement on authentic assessment* (pp. 112-113). New York, NY: Macmillan/McGraw-Hill.

Spandel, V., & Stiggins, R. J. (1990). *Creating writers: Linking assessment and writing instruction.* New York, NY: Longman.

SECTION IV: CONCLUSION

Chapter 13

KEEPING IT GOING

Teachers Engaged in Learning

The following vignettes give examples of how teachers may go through the process of change, in order to make balanced literacy instruction a reality in their classrooms. Both cases show the importance of colleagues in supporting the process of change.

A New Teacher Focuses on the Writers' Workshop

Marilyn Smith was starting her second year in the classroom. She had found her first year quite a struggle, although she had managed in the second semester to introduce a writers' workshop to her sixth graders. This year Marilyn wanted to start her writers' workshop right away. She made plans to work with Alison Lee, a resource teacher at her school. When Marilyn approached her, Alison said she would be happy to come to the classroom to observe, to assist with writing conferences, and to offer suggestions. Alison's schedule allowed her to visit Marilyn's classroom once every two weeks.

Alison and Marilyn sat down to go over a copy of the implementation checklist for the writers' workshop shown in Figure 13.1 of this chapter (Figure 13.2 presents the parallel implementation checklist for the readers' workshop). Marilyn felt that all the items were appropriate for her classroom, and that she would like to use the checklist to help her set goals. Marilyn

Figure 13.1   READERS' WORKSHOP IMPLEMENTATION CHECKLIST (CONT'D.)

STUDENT OPPORTUNITIES
(Has the teacher created an environment where most students can...?)

	Oct	Nov	Dec	Jan	Feb	Mar	Apr	May
Ownership of Process:								
Enjoy reading								
Show confidence/pride								
Goals:								
Set goals								
Reflect on goals								
Evaluate progress								
Value the reading process								
Reading Community Member:								
Join teacher led discussion								
Discuss reading w/ peers								
Knowledge of Reading Process:								
Read for a purpose								
Use word reading strategies								
Use voc. dev. strategies								
Show personal response to lit								
Comprehend story elements								
Construct theme								
Make life connection								
Understand reasons behind process								
Knowledge of Gr. Benchmarks								
Independence as Reader								

Figure 13.2 WRITERS' WORKSHOP IMPLEMENTATION CHECKLIST

CLASSROOM ORGANIZATION

	Oct	Nov	Dec	Jan	Feb	Mar	Apr	May
Frequency (average 4-5 times per week)								
Length (minimum 45 minutes per day)								
Workshop Rules/Procedure:								
Collaborative decisions								
Clarity and consistency								
Materials:								
Accessibility								
Amount								
Variation								
References/Resources:								
Accessibility								
Variety of types								
Regular location for:								
Large group sharing								
Conferring								
Quiet work								
Editing								
Publishing								
Promoting collaboration								
Student Publications:								
Variety of genres								
Variety of formats								
Regularly published								
Accessible								
Use in instruction								
Writing Folders/Notebooks:								
Contents:								
Work-in-progress								
Record keeping forms								
Items show organization								
Filing system:								
Drafts								
Published with drafts								
Student Portfolios:								
Contents:								
Writting samples								
Record keeping forms								
Meetings with teacher								

went over the checklist and marked the items that she felt she already had in place. These had mainly to do with scheduling and the physical arrangement of her classroom. For the first month, Marilyn decided her goal would be to give mini-lessons on classroom procedures. These would include teaching the students how to conduct peer conferences. Alison agreed that this was a good place to start.

The following Wednesday, Alison came to observe Marilyn's writers' workshop. Marilyn had planned her mini-lesson well, but it lasted nearly 20 minutes. When the time came for the students to begin writing, they had difficulty settling down. Alison and Marilyn both circulated around the room, conducting brief conferences. Alison noticed that Marilyn had excellent rapport with her students. Just as all the students seemed to be getting involved in their writing, the recess bell rang.

At recess, Alison asked Marilyn how she felt the writers' workshop had gone that morning. Marilyn replied that she thought the students had gotten restless because her lesson had gone on too long. Once they started writing, the students seemed noisy and restless. Alison agreed with these observations. Marilyn said she would work on keeping her mini-lessons brief, no longer than 10 minutes, so that the students could begin writing sooner. Alison suggested that, after the mini-lesson, Marilyn have five minutes of sustained silent writing, in order to help the students calm down and focus. Marilyn liked this idea and said she would give it a try.

The next time Alison observed, Marilyn kept her mini-lesson to 10 minutes. Then Marilyn had her students engage in sustained silent writing for five minutes. She circulated around the room to help the students get settled. The approach seemed to help the students concentrate. After sustained silent writing, the students were free to confer with one another, continue drafting, revise, or edit. Marilyn and Alison stationed themselves in different parts of the room and held conferences with individual students. Marilyn told Alison she felt her workshop was running more smoothly. She was limiting her mini-lessons to 10 minutes, and some of the students seemed able to conduct effective conferences with their peers.

At the end of the month, Alison and Marilyn met after school, and Marilyn completed the reflection and goal-setting form shown in Figure 13.3. Marilyn felt her goals for the past month had been accomplished, and that she wanted to move toward the goals of writing with her students and sharing her own writing. Marilyn thought that, instead of circulating around the room during sustained silent writing, she could sit down and write in her own notebook. This change would help her to reach her goal of writing with her students. Alison suggested that Marilyn sit with a different table of students each day, so everyone in the class would have a chance to see her write.

Figure 13.3 PROFESSIONAL DEVELOPMENT REFLECTION AND GOAL-SETTING FORM

Professional Development Reflection and Goal-Setting Form

Name _____

Date _____

1. I feel the following are going well in my classroom:

2. I have accomplished the following goals:

3. My current goals (continued from last time or new this time) are:

4. The kinds of support I could use to reach my current goals are:

Reflections:

Experienced Teachers Focus on the Readers' Workshop

Angie Diaz had been a teacher for 18 years. She had tried various grade levels but had decided that first grade was her favorite. Angie had the reputation for being an innovative teacher and was regarded as a leader at her school. This year, Angie's goal was to conduct an excellent readers' workshop. Angie's district favored literature-based instruction, as did her principal. However, unlike Marilyn, Angie did not have a resource teacher to work with her. Furthermore, due to budget cuts, the district was not offering any workshops on literature-based instruction.

Another first-grade teacher, Gail Heinrich, and a second-grade teacher, Donna Fleming, shared Angie's interest in the readers' workshop. Together, they decided to map out plans for their own professional development. The group decided to meet once a week after school. The time shifted from week to week, and sometimes the group was not able to meet at all. However, they kept in touch through brief conversations and evening phone calls.

At their first meeting, the members of the group discussed their concerns. Angie began by saying that she felt she was successful with most of her first graders but needed to find more time to promote the decoding ability of the struggling readers. She wanted to develop a schedule that would allow her to provide more small group instruction during her readers' workshop. Gail said she shared Angie's concerns but was not as far along in her understanding of the readers' workshop. She wanted to learn more about shared reading from Angie, in particular, how to teach phonics lessons with big books. Donna described her main concern as meeting the needs of all her students. She had some students whose literacy was still emergent and others who could read at the fourth-grade level. She wanted ideas for organizing her readers' workshop to address this wide range. She said she too would be interested in learning more about shared reading, since her class included four emergent readers. After further discussion, the group decided that their first goal would be to work on the overall organization of their readers' workshops. After that, they would turn to the question of small group instruction and shared reading in particular.

Angie had copies of a number of checklists for the readers' workshop, including the one shown in Figure 13.2. The teachers decided to devise their own checklist, using the one in Figure 13.2 as a model. Donna, a computer whiz, offered to produce clean copies of the checklist. At the next meeting, each of the teachers sat down with a copy of the checklist and marked off the items she felt were already in place in her classroom. Each also identified the items in the classroom organization section of the checklist that she wanted to focus on for the coming month. The teachers then discussed their goals with one another.

The teachers did not have the ability to observe in one another's classrooms, but they decided that they would move their meetings around to different classrooms. This would enable them to gain a better sense of what the others were doing. Since they were in Angie's room, Angie offered to share the schedule she was trying for her readers' workshop. She also gave a guided tour of her room, including the classroom library, computer area, and center for small group instruction. On subsequent occasions the group met in Gail's room and Donna's room, then returned to Angie's room again.

At the beginning of each month, the teachers took the first 10 minutes of the meeting to complete their reflection and goal-setting forms (see Figure 13.3). Sometimes they had the same goals, and sometimes they pursued individual goals.

The teachers had somewhat different systems for tracking their professional development. Angie had a large three-ring binder in which she kept her checklist, reflection forms, and articles on literature-based instruction and related topics. Angie took notes during the meetings, and she kept these notes in her binder. Gail kept a manila folder for the meetings and also brought along her writers' notebook. Her notebook included reflections on her teaching as well as other reflections. She often copied quotations from professional books and articles into her notebook. Donna, too, kept her materials in a manila folder. She preferred to write on the computer, and she sometimes read printouts of her electronic journal entries to the group. ✳

The Process of Change

A *paradigm shift* involves a change from one world view to another. Such a shift is currently taking place in the field of literacy instruction, as educators move from a focus on the transmission of skills to a focus on meaningful activities with embedded skill instruction (Au & Carroll, 1996; Carroll, Wilson, & Au, 1996). The process of moving toward balanced literacy instruction—including the writers' workshop, the readers' workshop, and portfolio assessment—can be lengthy and often involves a good deal of soul-searching.

One constraint on change is that not everyone is ready to change at the same time. Lea Ridley (1990) worked as a reading and writing consultant helping teachers move toward whole language. She encountered teachers with three different stances toward change: (a) proponents of the whole language philosophy, (b) those interested primarily in applications of whole language, and (c) those interested neither in philosophy nor applications. As Ridley learned, teachers in a given school seldom have the same readiness for change, whether they are moving toward whole language or another philosophy. At the outset, participants should recognize that people will be at various places along a continuum of change, and that different kinds of professional development activities will be appropriate for different groups.

Au and Scheu (1996) argue for the strategy of *going with the goers*. They believe that majority of resources professional development should be dedicated to the *goers*, the teachers most willing and able to take new ideas to heart and to make immediate changes in their practices. Once these teachers have become knowledgeable of the new ideas and practices, they can serve as models for other teachers. In this way precious resources for professional development are put to optimal use, and a firm foundation can be established for lasting change.

The strategy of going with the goers contrasts with the strategy of *spreading resources equally among all teachers*. This strategy is based on the belief that all teachers should receive the same opportunities for professional development at the same time. For example, the district may give a workshop and require everyone to attend. This strategy ignores the fact that teachers who are not yet ready to change may resent being forced to do so. As a consequence, they may actively resist attempts to promote change. A sensible approach might be to keep these teachers informed of workshops and other professional development events but not to compel their participation. As they see other teachers succeed with the new approaches, these teachers may become more willing to engage in the change process.

Initial Discussions

Suppose that a group of goers has been identified. What steps might members of this group take to move forward? A first step might be to begin with discussions of philosophy and the reasons for making changes. Questions for structuring the discussions include the following:

- What beliefs do members of the group hold about literacy, teaching, and learning?

- What do they hope to accomplish by bringing about change in their classrooms?

Members of the group do not have to come to a consensus about these issues. Rather, the purpose of the discussion is to give individuals the chance to make their beliefs, assumptions, and goals explicit. If notes are taken at each meeting, the group can gradually refine its goals and instructional philosophy.

The four articles in Chapter 1 will prove useful as background reading during these discussions. Each article is short enough to be read and discussed in the course of an after-school meeting. Participants may also follow a jigsaw approach. The group counts off from one to four. All the "ones" read the article on Strickland, the "twos" read the article on Vygotsky, and so on. After reading, the participants form jigsaw groups, with a one, two, three, and four in each group. Participants share the key ideas they gained from their reading with those who read different articles.

Choosing a Focus

Once the goers have discussed their beliefs and goals, they are ready for the next step, which is to select a focus for change. Teachers should choose to focus either on the writers' workshop and the process approach to writing, or on the readers' workshop and literature-based instruction. All teachers in the group need not choose the same focus. Au and Scheu (1996) found that teachers were more likely to be successful if they concentrated on one workshop at a time. Most teachers in their study chose to begin with the writers' workshop. The teachers did not neglect reading or other curriculum areas but continued to teach these subjects in much the same way as they had before. Making the decision to keep their teaching in other areas the same freed them to concentrate on making changes in the writers' workshop. Having a focus on just one of the workshops helped teachers to keep from feeling overwhelmed and allowed them to develop a thorough knowledge of their chosen workshop.

At this point, teachers whose states, districts, or schools are focusing on standards, outcomes, or benchmarks may wish to identify their major goals for student learning, either in reading or writing. Developing about five broad goals provides a good start. For ideas, refer to Reading Benchmarks (Chapter 11) and Writing Benchmarks (Chapter 12).

Participants who choose to focus on the readers' workshop will find it helpful to read and discuss Chapters 2 through 5. Those who choose to focus on the writers' workshop will find Chapters 6 through 9 informative. None of the chapters needs to be read straight through. Rather, participants should feel free to pick and choose among the articles, depending on the issues they find themselves facing in their classrooms. The articles highlighting the work of a particular educator—such as Violet Harris, Marie Clay, Donald Graves, or Lucy Calkins—provide background on theory and research. Other articles, while alluding to the research, address practical concerns, such as classroom organization and scheduling, or describe instructional strategies and activities.

Chapters 10, 11, and 12 on evaluating students' progress in the readers' and writers' workshops will prove useful after changes have been made in instruction. Beginning the change process with a focus on evaluation is not recommended. Changing the form of evaluation, without first improving students' learning opportunities through changes in instruction, generally does not lead to the desired increases in students' literacy achievement (Au, 1994).

Working Toward Full Implementation

Once the change process is underway, it is essential for teachers to keep on track and work toward full implementation of their chosen workshop. Au and Scheu (1996) found that improvements in student learning did not occur until teachers had fully implemented their chosen focus. Their findings point to the importance of staying with a particular focus for a least a year and possibly two or three years.

Teachers need to define what will constitute full implementation in the context of their particular classroom and school. Often, full implementation is best described in terms of a checklist, such as those presented in Figures 13.1 and 13.2. As shown in the vignettes earlier in this chapter, teachers may refer to these and other checklists, such as those developed by Johnson and Wilder (1992) and Vogt (1991). They probably will not adopt an existing checklist in its entirety, but will develop their own checklist for the writers' workshop or readers' workshop drawing on existing examples as sources of ideas. Once the checklist has been devised, teachers sit down and evaluate their teaching practices, noting which items are already in place in their classrooms and which items are not. At this point, they may find it helpful to use the reflection and goal-setting form shown in Figure 13.3. As illustrated in the vignettes, they set goals for the coming month by identifying the items they would like to work on. New goals are set and pursued until teachers feel that all checklist items are in place in their classrooms. A pair or small group of teachers may choose to work on the same items together, providing one another with ideas, and teachers may arrange to visit one another's classrooms. At this point the key to sustaining change may be the formation of formal and informal networks of teachers assisting one another.

In conclusion, while the process of change is always challenging, it can be made manageable if teachers keep a clear focus. The change process is facilitated if teachers can count on their colleagues for support through discussion groups and networks. Patience is required, as the change to new forms of literacy instruction and assessment is often a matter of years rather than months. Yet the benefits experienced by teachers and students can make all the hard work worthwhile. Teachers report new enthusiasm for teaching and a commitment to continue with innovative forms of instruction. Best of all, teachers see that they are able to develop students' ownership of literacy, as well as their ability to read and write. ✳

References

Au, K. H. (1994). Portfolio assessment: Experiences at the Kamehameha Elementary Education Program. In S. W. Valencia, E. H. Hiebert, & P. P. Afflerbach (Eds.), *Authentic reading assessment: Practices and possibilities* (pp. 103-126). Newark, DE: International Reading Association.

Au, K. H., & Carroll, J. H. (1996). Current research on classroom instruction: Goals, teachers' actions, and assessment. In D. Speece & B. Keogh (Eds.), *Research on classroom ecologies: Implications for inclusion of children with learning disabilities* (pp. 17-37). Hillsdale, NJ: Erlbaum.

Au, K. H., & Scheu, J. A. (1996). Journey toward holistic instruction. *The Reading Teacher, 49* (6), 468-477.

Carroll, J. H., Wilson, R. A., & Au, K. H. (1996). Explicit instruction in the context of the readers' and writers' workshops. In E. McIntyre & M. Pressley (Eds.), *Skills and strategies in whole language* (pp. 39-63). Norwood, MA: Christopher-Gordon.

Johnson, J. S., & Wilder, S. L. (1992). Changing reading and writing programs through staff development. *The Reading Teachers, 45* (8), 626-631.

Ridley, L. (1990). Enacting change in elementary school programs: Implementing a whole language perspective. *The Reading Teacher, 43* (9), 640-646.

Vogt, M. (1991). An observation guide for supervisors and administrators: Moving toward integrated reading/language arts instruction. *The Reading Teacher, 45* (3), 206-211.

Biographical Sketches

Dr. Kathryn Au

Kathryn H. Au is an associate professor in the College of Education at the University of Hawaii. Previously, she worked as a researcher, curriculum developer, teacher educator, and classroom teacher at the Kamehameha Elementary Program (KEEP) in Honolulu. Her research interest is the school literacy development of students of diverse cultural and linguistic backgrounds, and she has published over 60 articles on this topic. Dr. Au has been elected president of the National Reading Conference and a vice president of the American Educational Research Association. She is an active member of the International Reading Association (IRA).

Jacquelin H. Carroll

Jacquelin H. Carroll is a curriculum developer, researcher, and evaluator in Honolulu. Currently, she is working at the Cultural Learning Center at Kaala on a Hawaiian Studies curriculum for high school students designated to link the study of Hawaiian culture, language, and history with course work and field work in anthropology, archeology, ecology, agriculture, and nutrition. Previously, Jackie was a curriculum researcher and developer for the Kamehameha Elementary Education Program (KEEP), where she focused on literacy development with upper elementary school students. She has been a classroom teacher at the elementary, intermediate, and high school levels, with an emphasis on reading and special education.

Judith M. Scheu

Judith M. Scheu currently teaches first grade at a private school in Honolulu. She has also taught preschoolers and second graders and worked as a primary grades remedial reading teacher in a federally funded program. Judy was a curriculum developer for 13 years with the Kamehameha Elementary Education Program (KEEP), where her work centered on enhancing the literacy growth of native Hawaiian children.

INDEX

Subject Index